DINOSAURS

STOMP CHOMP & ROAR

Pam Manning

DINOSAURS
STOMP CHOMP & ROAR

By Pam Manning

Edited by Judy Pearlstein

Tech edit by Christina DeArmond

Design by Brian Grubb

Photographs by Aaron Leimkuehler

Illustrations by Lon Eric Craven

Production Assistance by Jo Ann Groves

Published by Kansas City Star Books
1729 Grand Boulevard
Kansas City, Missouri 64108

First edition, first printing
ISBN: 978-1-933466-69-9

Printed in the United States of America
By Walsworth Publishing Co.
Marceline, Missouri

**To order copies, call StarInfo,
816-234-4636 (say "Operator)**

KANSAS CITY STAR BOOKS
Kansas City, Missouri

KANSAS CITY STAR QUILTS
Continuing the Tradition

PickleDish.com
The Quilter's Home Page

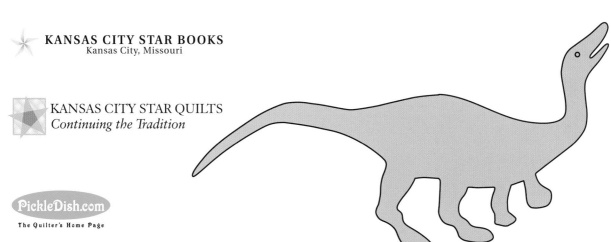

Acknowledgements

First I must thank my husband, Don, for making my life so blessed that I can take the time to quilt and then write a book. You are my faithful soul mate and I love you always! Thank you also to my daughter, Karen, my best friend! It's so helpful to bounce ideas off you.

Thank you to my grandsons, Jaron and Levi, for teaching me to love dinosaurs and for lending your favorite dinosaurs for the photo shoot. You are my joy!

Judy Pearlstein, you always surprise me with your eye for consistency. You truly make a book come together. I am indebted to you also, Diane McClendon, for opening your home for the cover photo. Many thanks to photographer Aaron Leimkuhler and designer Brian Grubb, for carrying all that was needed to set up and shoot the photo. You all went beyond duty's call and I am indebted and call you friends!

Thank you to Lon Eric Craven for making my templates look wonderful. (Your dinosaur creations are amazing too! Thank you Doug Weaver for fitting this book into the crowded schedule you had this summer. What an encouragement!

And last, but always first in my life, I want to thank the Lord for His wonderful love.

P.S.

"Thanks also to all who had a helping hand in making this quilt book special and to all the quilters who will one day make this quilt for someone they love. May you and yours be blessed!"

Table of Contents

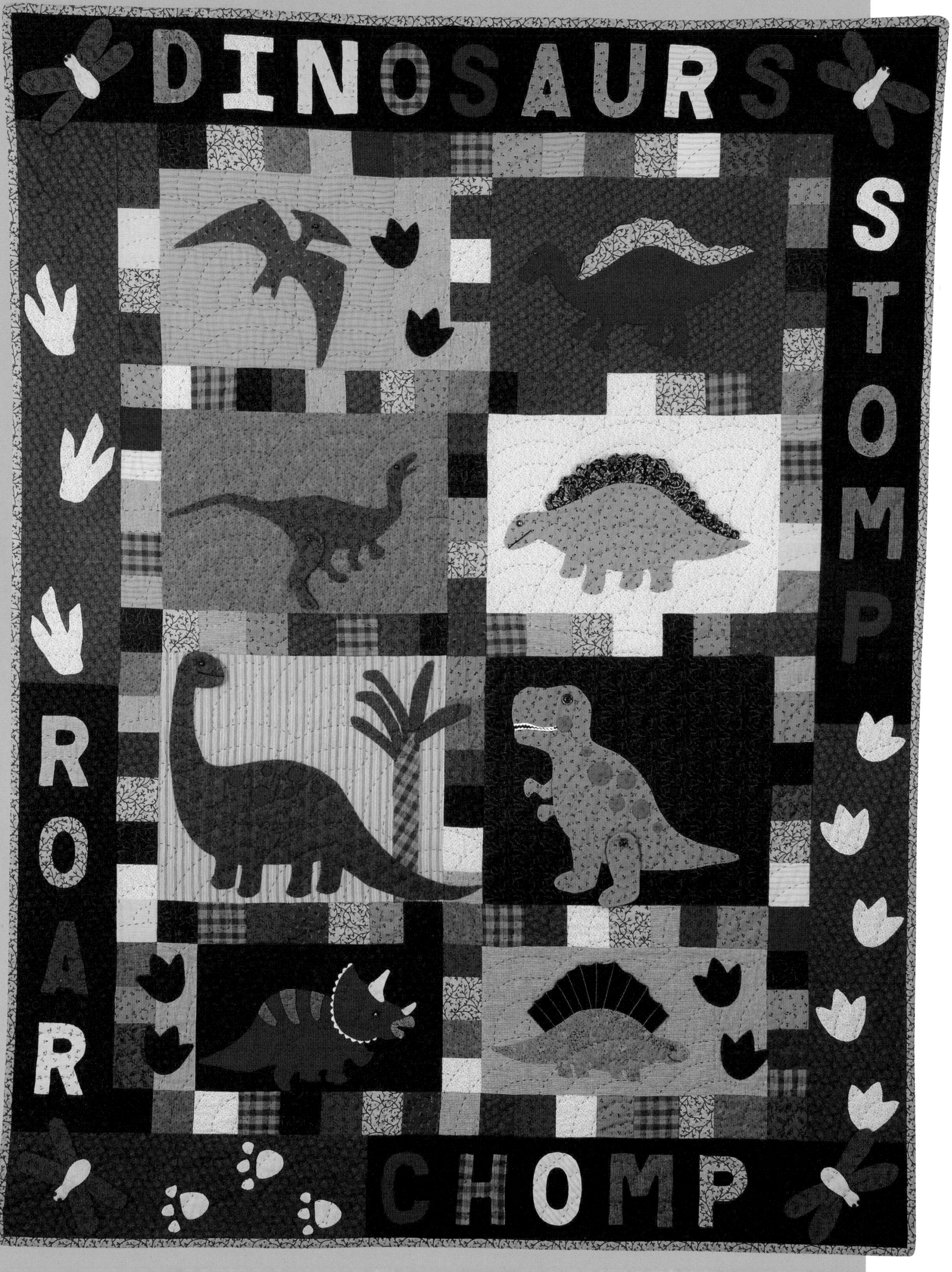
DINOSAURS
STOMP
ROAR
CHOMP

Glossary

Appliqué Techniques

Here are two appliqué techniques that I enjoy doing. The second one is good for needle appliqué as well as machine appliqué.

Technique #1

Trace all your appliqué pattern pieces onto the dull side of freezer paper. Also transfer any pertinent markings such as spots or eye, mouth or limb placement at this time. Cut out on the line. Press the shiny side to the right side of your appliqué fabric. Cut $1/4''$ away from your pattern piece.

When you are ready to appliqué, mark with a chalk pencil, etc., next to the freezer paper. Fabric glue your pattern piece to the background with any acid free washable glue. When you are ready to start your appliqué, clip your concave (inside) curves close to the seam line (but not too close). Remove the freezer paper and needleturn your appliqué piece in position. Use a $12'' - 18''$ thread the same color as your appliqué piece. Come up through the underside of your background fabric and out through the fold of your appliqué seam. Using the tip and shaft of your needle, turn in your seam allowance. Go into your background fabric opposite your thread in the appliqué piece, coming up again $1/8''$ from your last stitch, a little under the seam fold and out through the fold, catching at least three threads. Repeat with your needle going back in again opposite where you came out. Keep your stitches $1/16'' - 1/8''$ apart (more stitches on curves and points and a few less on straight seams). Snug your thread as you go. (If it puckers it's too tight.)

Technique #2:

Trace all your appliqué pattern pieces onto the shiny side of freezer paper, along with any pertinent markings. Cut out on the line. Press the shiny side to the wrong side of your appliqué fabric. Cut $1/4''$ away from the pattern piece. When you are ready to assemble your block, spray a small amount of fabric starch into a medicine cup, etc., and with a small paint brush, wet your seam allowance but don't get it so wet that your freezer paper gets wet. Press your seam allowance onto the freezer paper following the seam line, until the whole block has the seam allowance turned under. Take your time and do a nice smooth job. When you are done, remove the freezer paper. Your seam allowance will stay in place and you are ready to assemble your block. When you are sure that the pieces that need to be tucked behind others are all in place, begin to glue it down with acid free, water soluble glue such as Roxanne's Glue Baste-it. Put tiny dots about an inch or two around your seam allowance and press with the iron. It will stay put until you are ready to appliqué.

BIG STITCH

This is a great stitch to use on primitive/folk art quilts and wall hangings. You can use a number of styles. The pattern is up to your imagination. For the large project, I used the Baptist Fan with arcs spaced 1 ½" apart. You can get stencils at most quilt shops. Mark the first small arc on the stencil and then skip two, mark the next, etc. (You will have five rows in each arc when done). Line the first arc up on the lower right hand side of your project and mark as many sets as you can get into your hoop (15-18" hoop). Start each row hereafter on the same edge. Use # 10 crochet cotton and a #5 crewel embroidery needle. Stitch ¼" up and ¼" under. You can let your knots be seen on the back as it gives your quilt a nice primitive look when it's finished. If you choose to do this, tie on the next thread with a 'surgeon knot' which is right over left twice around and left over right, twice around and tighten. Leave about a ¾" tail.

SLIP STITCH

Working from right to left, knot your thread and bring the needle and thread out through one folded edge. For the first and each succeeding stitch, slip the needle in through the fold just opposite where the thread came out in the last stitch and bring it out about ⅛" and pull the thread through. Continue to slip the needle and thread through the opposing folded edges every eighth of an inch. (The experts say ¼" is good but I have always done it ⅛" as I like the look of it better.)

STITCH IN THE DITCH

"Stitch-in-the ditch" does not necessarily mean you actually stitch in or on the seam line in this case, but get as close as you can and use a matching thread so your seam will disappear into the background. Don't sew onto the dinosaur body. You are just reinforcing your appliqué stitch on the dinosaurs with moving parts that can be grabbed by little fingers and pulled.

QUILTING COTTON

Unless you are doing an art quilt, you should use 100% cotton in your quilts. Good quality cotton is more enjoyable to work with and shrinks and frays less. One bad piece of fabric in the quilt can ruin the whole quilt over time.

SUPPLY LIST FOR YOUR DINOSAUR QUILT

Quilt size: 66 ½" x 86"

Fabric yardage and color:
- 1 yard black
- ¼ yard and fat quarter 2nd black
- ½ yard and fat quarter of dark green
- 1 fat quarter 3rd black
- 1 fat quarter brown/black stripe
- 1 fat quarter med. brown
- 1 fat quarter brown
- 2 fat quarters red/black
- 1 fat quarter red/cream
- 1 fat quarter red
- 3 fat quarters dark greens
- 1 fat quarter cream
- 2 fat quarters light green
- 2 fat quarters gold
- 1 fat quarter gold/black stripe

SCRAPS: (I define a scrap as less than 1/8th of a yard.)

- 1 purple
- 2 dark green
- 1 black
- 1 small green/black check
- 1 dark brown/black stripe

NOTIONS

- Six ¼" round ball black buttons
- Three ½" flat round dark brown buttons
- One ¾" flat round dark brown button
- One ⅔" flat round dark brown button
- Eight size 2/0 black snaps
- 8" of ¼" wide white rickrack
- 10" of ½" wide light green rickrack
- Red and black 3-ply embroidery floss
- Cotton thread to match your appliqué pieces

HINTS:

To give you full size pattern pieces, I have, of necessity, broken them up into sections. You will assemble them together as you make your template for each block. You will see on these pieces that I have labeled them with a letter (each quilt block has a different letter A-L) and a number for each different pattern piece.

Some of the dinos in this quilt have 3D parts (parts of them set away from the quilt).

When the pattern piece calls for you to cut two pieces that will be sewn together and turned right side out, I cut one pattern of freezer paper, lay two fabric pieces right sides together, iron on the freezer paper and cut one time. Leaving the freezer paper on, I sew next to the seam allowance and then remove the paper. You should reinforce these pieces with extra machine 'stitching in the ditch' as they will get extra tugs and pulls from your little guys.

Meaning of name: "The winged toothless one."

Wingspan: 25-33' Height: 6' tall at the hips
Weight: 55 lbs.
Food: Fish and bugs
First fossil found: 1876 in Smoky Hill River,
Wallace County, Kansas, USA

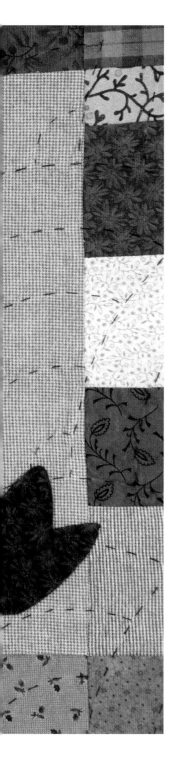

PTERANODON

(ter-AN-o-DON)

Finished block size is 13 ½″ X 21″.

FABRIC AND NOTION REQUIREMENTS

- ○ 1 fat quarter of medium brown for background A
- ○ 1 fat quarter of dark green for Pteranodon
- ○ 13″ x 5″ red/cream check for background Aa
- ○ 4 ½″ x 9″ of black for I - footprints
- ○ ¼″ round black button

BLOCK CONSTRUCTION

Add seam allowance on all appliqué pieces when cutting.
- ○ Cut: 15″ x 18 ½″ background A from medium brown.
- ○ Cut: 15″ x 4 ½″ background Aa from red/cream check.
- ○ Cut one of piece A1, green (assemble pattern) and two of piece I (footprints), black. (p. 31)
- ○ Center A1 onto background A and appliqué.
- ○ Sew right side of background A and left side Aa together to make background 15″ x 22 ½″.
- ○ Appliqué two of I (fossil footprint). See photo for placement.
- ○ Add mouth using the outline stitch with red 3-ply floss. Use pattern for placement. (p. 42)
- ○ Sew button for eye where pattern indicates.
- ○ Press and trim block to 14″ x 21 ½″. (Trim from left side of block).

OURANOSAURUS

(oo-RAHN-o-SAWR-us)

Finished block size is 13 ½" x 21".

FABRIC AND NOTION REQUIREMENTS

- ○ 1 fat quarter of dark green for background
- ○ 1 fat quarter of red/black for body
- ○ 1 fat quarter gold for spine
- ○ ¼" round black button

BLOCK CONSTRUCTION

Add seam allowance on all appliqué pieces when cutting.

- ○ Cut 15" x 22 ½" dark green background.
- ○ Cut one of piece B1 red/black (assemble pattern), and two of piece B2 gold.
- ○ Sew B2, right sides together, around top curves between dots. Clip to seam and trim any bulk. Turn right side out and press well. Baste bottom closed ⅛" — ¼" inch from edge. Clip to basting.
- ○ Glue your 14 ¼" B2 to the top of B1, lining up your marks. (turning your ¼" seam on B1 to the inside).
- ○ Appliqué B1 to the center of the background through B2. (Do not sew the top of B2 to the background. You may tack it in a couple places later if you like.)
- ○ When finished, stitch in the ditch along the seam where B1 and B2 meet to reinforce the seam, being careful not to sew up onto B1.
- ○ Add mouth, using the outline stitch with black 3-ply floss. Use pattern for placement.
- ○ Sew button for eye where pattern indicates.
- ○ Press and trim block to 14" x 21 ½".

Meaning of name: "Valiant lizard"

Length: 23" Height: 16.5'
Weight: 660 lbs.
Food: plants
First fossil found: 1976 in Niger, Africa

Meaning of name: "Egg stealer"

Length: 6 — 8'
Weight: 55 — 76 lbs.
Food: Originally thought to be an egg eater, this dinosaur has been recently
reclassified as a nurturer and plant eater.
First found in 1924 in the Gobi desert in Mongolia.

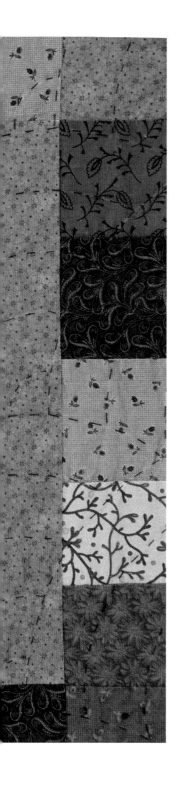

OVIRAPTOR

(OH-vi-RAP-tor)

Finished block size is 14" x 21".

FABRIC AND NOTION REQUIREMENTS

- ❍ 1 fat quarter of dark green for background C
- ❍ 1 fat quarter of red/black for body C1 and C2
- ❍ ½" flat round dark button
- ❍ ¼" round black button

BLOCK CONSTRUCTION

Add seam allowance on all appliqué pieces when cutting.

- ❍ Cut 15 ½" x 22 ½" of dark green background.
- ❍ Cut one of C1 red/black (assemble pattern) and two of C2 red/black.
- ❍ Sew C2, right sides together (leaving an opening to turn).
- ❍ Clip to seam and trim any bulk. Turn right side out and press well. Slip stitch the opening closed. See glossary for technique. (Topstitch ¼" from edge.)
- ❍ Sew leg in place with ½" flat button where pattern indicates.
- ❍ Sew button for eye where pattern indicates.
- ❍ Press and trim block to 14 ½" x 21 ½".

STEGOSAURUS

(STEG-o-SAWR-us)

Finished block size is 14" x 21".

FABRIC AND NOTION REQUIREMENTS

- ❍ 1 fat quarter of cream for background D
- ❍ 1 fat quarter of light green for D1 body
- ❍ $\frac{1}{8}$ yard or half a fat quarter of black for spikes
- ❍ $\frac{1}{2}$" flat round black button

BLOCK CONSTRUCTION

Add seam allowance on all appliqué pieces when cutting.

- ❍ Cut 15 $\frac{1}{2}$ x 22 $\frac{1}{2}$" of cream background

The spikes on this dino's back are 3D. So where it calls for "Cut 4", you will put two pieces of fabric face to face and cut two sets.

- ❍ Cut one of D1 (assemble pattern), D11 and D12, light green.
- ❍ Cut four of D4, D7, D9 and D10, black.
- ❍ Cut eight of D1/D8, D2/D6, and D3/D5, black.
- ❍ Sew two spikes each of D4, D7, D9 and D10, black.
- ❍ Sew four spikes each of D1/D8, D2/D6, and D3/D5, black.
- ❍ Clip to seam and trim any bulk. Turn right side out and press well. Make two rows of spikes, basting in numerical order, $\frac{1}{8}$" from edge. Leave a space between each spike with your basting thread (about $\frac{1}{2}$") and gather each spike. Both rows of spikes should be about 15" long.
- ❍ Place the second row (as in pattern on pages 36-37) on top of the first row but offset it half a spike. Baste these two rows together. They should measure 15 $\frac{1}{2}$".
- ❍ Baste or fabric glue your 15 $\frac{1}{2}$" staggered row of spikes to the top of D1 between the marks.
- ❍ Appliqué D1 to center of the background. When finished, stitch in the ditch (see glossary) along the seam where D1 and D9 meet, to reinforce the seam.
- ❍ Add mouth using the outline stitch with black 3-ply floss. Use pattern for placement.
- ❍ Sew button for eye where pattern indicates.
- ❍ Press and trim block to 14 $\frac{1}{2}$" x 21 $\frac{1}{2}$".

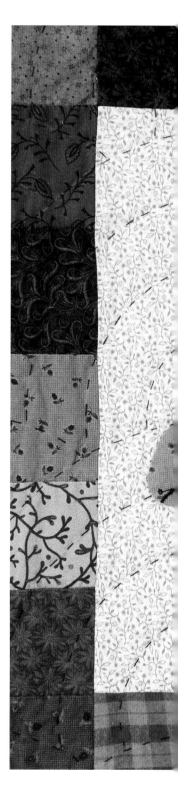

Meaning of name: "Plated lizard"

Length: 26-29' Height: 9' at hips
Weight: 2-3 tons
Food: Plants
First fossil found: 1876 in Colorado, USA

Meaning of name: Arm lizard
Length: 80-85' Height: 23'
Weight: 33-88 tons
Food: Plants
First fossil found: 1900 in the Grand River Valley in western Colorado, USA.
Later found in Tanzania, Africa and North America

16

BRACHIOSAURUS

(BRACK-ee-o-SAWR-us)

Finished block size is 17 ½" x 21"

FABRIC AND NOTION REQUIREMENTS

- ○ ½ yard gold/brown stripe for background E
- ○ ½ yard dark green for E1 and E1a body
- ○ 3 x 5" scrap of red for spots, gold/black plaid for trunk, and
  4 ½" X 13" of 2nd green for leaves
- ○ Two ¼" round black buttons
- ○ 3-ply black floss for mouth

BLOCK CONSTRUCTION

Add seam allowance on all appliqué pieces when cutting.

- ○ Cut 19" x 22 ½" of gold/brown stripe for background.

- ○ Cut one each of E1 (assemble pattern), and E1a from dark green. Transfer marks from pattern. The head is three-dimensional and is not appliquéd to the background. Sew E1 and E1a, right sides together from the line on one side, around to the line on the other side. Clip to seam and trim any bulk. Turn right side out and press well.

- ○ Cut one E2, two of E3 and three of E4 from red scrap. Appliqué spots to the dino as on the pattern piece.

- ○ Cut one each of E5 — E9 from 2nd dark green scrap.

- ○ Cut a gold/black plaid 2 ½" x 12 ½" strip, on the diagonal, for the tree trunk. Appliqué to background 2" from finished edge, tucking E8 behind trunk on top (follow page 43 for placement of branches). Appliqué E5 — E7 green leaves as in diagram.

- ○ Appliqué E9 to within 1" of edge. You will finish E9 when you add the border.

- ○ Appliqué E1, the dino, to the background. Use photo for placement. (Stop at tail 1" from the edge. You will finish his tail when you put the first border on, and remember you will be trimming ½" off each side when this block is finished.) Head will not be appliquéd down. Tuck your seams from the head to the inside. Reinforce by stitching twice on the line. (Use your machine. Brac's head will get lots of loving tugs).

- ○ Add mouth using the outline stitch with black 3-ply floss on both sides of head. Use pattern for placement. (p. 42)

- ○ Sew two buttons for eyes where the pattern indicates (or embroider a sleeping eye on one side, page 42).

- ○ Press and trim to 18" x 21 ½".

TYRANNOSAURUS REX

(tie-RAN-uh-SAW-rus REKS)

Finished block size is 17 ½" x 21"

FABRIC AND NOTION REQUIREMENTS

- ½ yard black for background
- 1 fat quarter brown for F1, F2, F7, F8 and F9 body
- 6" square of purple for F3, F4, F5 and F6 spots
- 8" of ¼" white rick rack for teeth
- ¾" and ⅔" flat round dark buttons

BLOCK CONSTRUCTION

Add seam allowance on all appliqué pieces when cutting.

- Cut 19" x 22 ½" of black for background F.

- Cut one of F1 (assemble pattern), F7, F8 and F9 and two of F2, right sides together, from brown.

- Cut one of F3, and two of F4, F5 and F6 from purple.

- Appliqué purple spots onto F1 using pattern for placement. (p. 44, 45. Leave spot F5 off mouth for now).

- Cut two 4" pieces of white rick rack. Sew off-center of rick rack (so just the bumps will show for the teeth) to inside of mouth tapering to a ⅛" seam. Clip inside the mouth to lay flat. Trim extra rick rack. (Spot F5 will hide any imperfections.)

- Baste or fabric glue F1 body to the center of the background. Remember to tuck F7 arm and F9 leg under F1 using pattern for placement.

- Appliqué F1 to the background. Stitch in the ditch (not on the body) between teeth and body for reinforcement.

- Appliqué F7 arm in place and F5 spot on mouth.

- Sew F2 leg, right sides together (leaving a 2" opening on back of leg to turn).

- Clip to seam and trim any bulk. Turn right side out and press well. Slip stitch the opening closed. See glossary for technique. Topstitch ¼" from edge.

- Sew leg in place with ⅔" flat button where pattern indicates.

- Sew ¾" button for eye where pattern indicates.

- Press and trim to 18" x 21 ½".

Meaning of name: Tyrant reptile

Length: 50′ Height: 15-20′ tall
Weight: 5-7 tons
Food: Meat eater
First fossil found: 1902 in Hell Creek, Montana, USA.

Meaning of name: Three horned face

Length: 30'   Height: 7' tall at hips
Weight: up to 6-12 tons
Food: Plants
First fossil found: 1988 in Western North America

TRICERATOPS

(try-SER-a-tops)

Finished block size is: 10 ½" x 21".

FABRIC AND NOTION REQUIREMENTS

- ○ 1 fat quarter black for background G
- ○ 13" x 5" scrap red/cream check for background Gg
- ○ 1 fat quarter red/black for body
- ○ 4 ½" x 9" black for footprints, 4" x 4" green for stripes, 3" x 3" gold for mouth, and 3" x 3" cream for horns
- ○ 10" light green rick rack for around head
- ○ ½" flat round black buttons

BLOCK CONSTRUCTION

Add seam allowance on all appliqué pieces when cutting.

- ○ Cut 12" x 19 ½" strip of black for background G.
- ○ Cut 12" x 3 ½" strip of red/cream check for background Gg. Join right sides together to make the background 12" x 22 ½".
- ○ Cut one of G1 body (assemble pattern), and 1 each of G2-G9 pieces.
- ○ Appliqué G3-G5 green stripes on the back of G1. See pattern for placement.
- ○ Cut 10" of ³⁄₈" green rick rack.
- ○ Baste or fabric glue body pieces G1 and G2 to the center of background G, gluing rick rack in place between G1 and G2 as on pattern and appliqué. Tuck the ends of rick rack to the underside.
- ○ Appliqué G6-G9 gold mouth and cream horns on G1. See pattern for placement.
- ○ Cut two of I footprints, black. (p. 31)
- ○ Appliqué both footprints onto red background Gg, stopping 1" from edge. You will finish appliqué when you add the first border. See photo for placement.
- ○ Sew on ½" button. See pattern for placement.
- ○ Press and trim to 11" x 21 ½". Trim on right side of background.

Meaning of name: "two measures of tooth"
(He is thought to be pre-dinosaur.)

Length: 11 feet
Weight: 550 lbs.
Food: Plants and meat
Found in TX and Oklahoma, USA and in Nova Scotia, Canada

DIMETRODON

(die-MET-roh-don)

Finished block size is: 10 ½" x 21".

FABRIC AND NOTION REQUIREMENTS

- ❍ 1 fat quarter light green for background H
- ❍ 1 fat quarter gold for H1 body
- ❍ 13" x 5" scrap red/cream check for background Hh
- ❍ 18" x 11" black for H2 sail
- ❍ 4 ½" x 9" 2nd black for I footprints
- ❍ ¼" round black button
- ❍ 3-ply floss, red for mouth

BLOCK CONSTRUCTION

Add seam allowance on all appliqué pieces when cutting.

- ❍ Cut 12" x 18 ¾" of green for background H.
- ❍ Cut 12" x 4 ¼" of red/cream check for background Hh. Join right sides together to make the background 12" x 22 ½" (Red is on the right).
- ❍ Cut one of H1 body from gold (assemble pattern), and 1 of H2 sail from black.
- ❍ Cut two of I footprints from black. (p. 31)
- ❍ Transfer the fold lines from H2 sail to your fabric. Press each fold. Now sew ¹⁄₁₆" away from the edge on each fold. (The closer to the edge you can sew, the nicer the sail will look.)

  Press your sail flat with the seams going the same direction. On the right side of the same color fabric, turn your finished sail face down and trace the shape of your sail. (Don't add a seam allowance.) Cut out your shape. With right sides together, sew about ¹⁄₈" around the sides and top of the sail.

  Clip the curves and turn right side out and press.

  Baste the bottom together ¹⁄₈" from the edge.
- ❍ Glue H1 dino over H2 sail in center of H green background, lining up your marks from the pattern piece. Appliqué all but top and sides of H2 sail. Tack top and ends of sail in a couple of places.
- ❍ Stitch in the ditch along the seam where H1 and H2 meet, to reinforce the seam. (Don't sew on the body.)
- ❍ Add mouth, using the outline stitch with red 3-ply floss. Use pattern for placement.
- ❍ Sew button for eye where pattern indicates.
- ❍ Appliqué two I fossil footprints from black onto red/cream check as in photo.
- ❍ Press and trim to 11" x 21 ½".

DINOSAURS
STOMP
ROAR
CHOMP

BORDERS AROUND BLOCKS A - H

FABRIC REQUIREMENTS

❍ 18 — 20 different colored scraps that you used in the body of the quilt

REMINDER:

Press as you go. Match your seams on all corner blocks.

BLOCK CONSTRUCTION

❍ Cut strips 3 ½" wide from 18 — 20 different colored scraps that you used in the quilt

❍ Cut blocks from these strips 1 ½" to 4 ½" long, making most of them 3 ½". Hint: Keep your 3 ½" going in one direction. Use these to make your border.

❍ Sew together three strips 3 ½" x 14". Sew to each side of block A and the right side of block B.

❍ Sew together three strips 3 ½" x 14 ½". Sew to each side of block C and the right side of block D.

❍ Sew together three strips 3 ½" x 18". Sew to each side of block E and the right side of block F.

❍ Sew together three strips 3 ½" x 11". Sew to each side of block G and the right side of block H.

❍ Sew ten strips 3 ½" x 21 ½".

❍ Add a block that measures 3 ½" square to each end of five of these 21 ½" strips. This strip will now measure 3 ½" X 27 ½". As you join all your blocks together, line up the seams on the end blocks. Sew to the tops of blocks A, C and E and the top and bottom of G.

❍ Add a block that measures 3 ½" square to the right side of the last five 21 ½" strips. This strip will now measure 3 ½" x 24 ½". Sew to the tops of blocks B, D and F and the top and bottom of H.

❍ Sew the right side of A, C, E and G to the left side of B, D, F and H .

❍ Sew the bottom of A/B to the top of C/D.

❍ Sew the bottom of C/D to the top of E/F.

❍ Sew the bottom of E/F to the top of G/H.

Press seams in one direction as you go.

OUTSIDE BORDERS

FABRIC AND NOTION REQUIREMENTS

❍ 1 yard main black

❍ ¾ yard dark green

❍ ⅜ yard of second black

❍ 1 fat quarter of red, orange, and tan

❍ Scraps of tan, light green, green, brown, red, brown plaid, dark. green and gold that you used in the quilt

❍ 8 size 2/0 black snaps

RIGHT SIDE BORDER • STOMP

Finished block size is: 70 ½" x 7 ¾"

BLOCK CONSTRUCTION

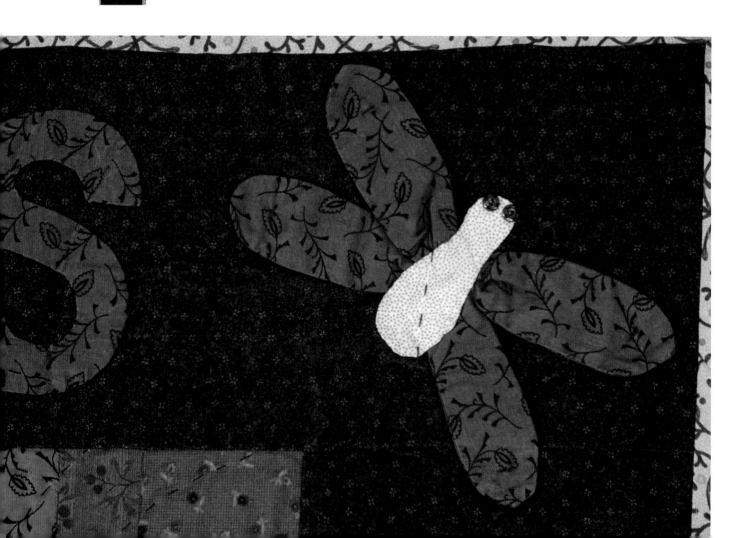

- Cut 42" x 8" of main black
- Cut 30" x 8" of green. Sew short ends together to make 71 ½" x 8".
- Cut out of scraps the letters for STOMP.
- Starting with the black end at the top, leave a space of 3 ½" and appliqué the S on. Hereafter leave 2 ½" between each letter. Appliqué letters STOMP as in photo.
- Cut five tan I footprints. Starting from the bottom edge of green, appliqué the five I footprints. Start 1" from the bottom edge and hereafter space 3" apart. Stagger them off-center to the right and left. See photo.
- Press and trim block to 71" x 8".
- Sew onto right side of quilt
- Press seam to outside.

LEFT SIDE BORDER ○ ROAR

Finished block size is: 70 ½″ x 7 ¾″

BLOCK CONSTRUCTION

- Cut 42″ x 8″ of dark green
- Cut 31″ x 8″ of second black. Sew short ends together to make 71 ½″ x 8″.
- Cut out of scraps the letters for ROAR.
- Appliqué the letter R, 2 ¼″ from the middle seam and space them 2 ¼″ apart hereafter.
- Appliqué three J footprints starting 1″ from the middle seam and space them 6″ apart hereafter.

Stagger them off-center to the right and left. See photo on page 24.

- Press and trim block to 71″ x 8″.
- Sew onto left side of quilt.
- Press seam to outside.

BOTTOM BORDER ○ CHOMP

Finished block size is: 66 ½″ x 7 ¾″

BLOCK CONSTRUCTION

- Cut 41 ½″ x 8″ of same black as top.
- Cut 26 ½″ x 8″ of dark green. Sew short ends together to make 67 ½″ x 8″.
- Cut three sets of fossil footprint K. Sew staggered 2″, 6″ and 12″ from the left side of the seam as in photo.
- Cut out of scraps the letters for CHOMP.
- Appliqué the letter C 1 ¾″ from the right side of the seam. Space the rest of the letters 1 ¾″ apart and appliqué on.
- For the four corner bugs, fold your red fabric with the right sides together. Cut 8 each (16 total) of wings M and N adding a ¼″ seam allowance. Sew a ¼″ seam around the curve following next to the freezer paper seam. Clip curve, trim bulk and turn right side out. Press. Baste each end and gather to ⅞″. (Keep M & N separate.) If you want to stuff the body with a little batting, make a small slit on the back of the quilt behind the appliqued body and add the batting. Sew it shut, but don't pucker the fabric.
- Cut 4 of body O.

❍ The head will face the outside corner and the M wings will be closest to the head.

See pattern on page 39 for placement.(Photo, p. 24)

❍ Center the bugs on each corner and sew on. (Repeat on the top border.)

❍ Sew two snaps on each bug for eyes.

❍ Sew border onto the bottom of the quilt.

❍ Press seam to the outside.

TOP BORDER ● DINOSAURS

Finished block size is: 66 ½″ x 7 ¾″.

Add seam allowance on all appliqué pieces when cutting.

BLOCK CONSTRUCTION

❍ Cut 41 ½″ x 8″ and 26 ½′ x 8″ from same black. Sew short ends together to make 67 ½″ x 8″.

❍ Cut out of scraps the letters for DINOSAURS.

❍ Appliqué the letter S in the center of your top. On each side of S appliqué your letters 1 ¾″ apart until you have spelled DINOSAURS.

❍ Press and trim to 66 ½″ x 8″.

❍ Sew onto the top of the quilt.

❍ Press seam to outside.

FINISHING QUILT

Finished back size is: 66 ½" x 86".

FABRIC REQUIREMENT

- 5 yards of 45" green quilt fabric
- Double bed size batting — I used wool.

BLOCK CONSTRUCTION

- Cut two 35" x 90" green backing pieces. Sew lengthways. Press.
- Sandwich the batting between the top and backing. Baste.
- Quilt using a Baptist Fan stencil and a ¼" Big Stitch.
  See glossary for technique.

PTERANODON

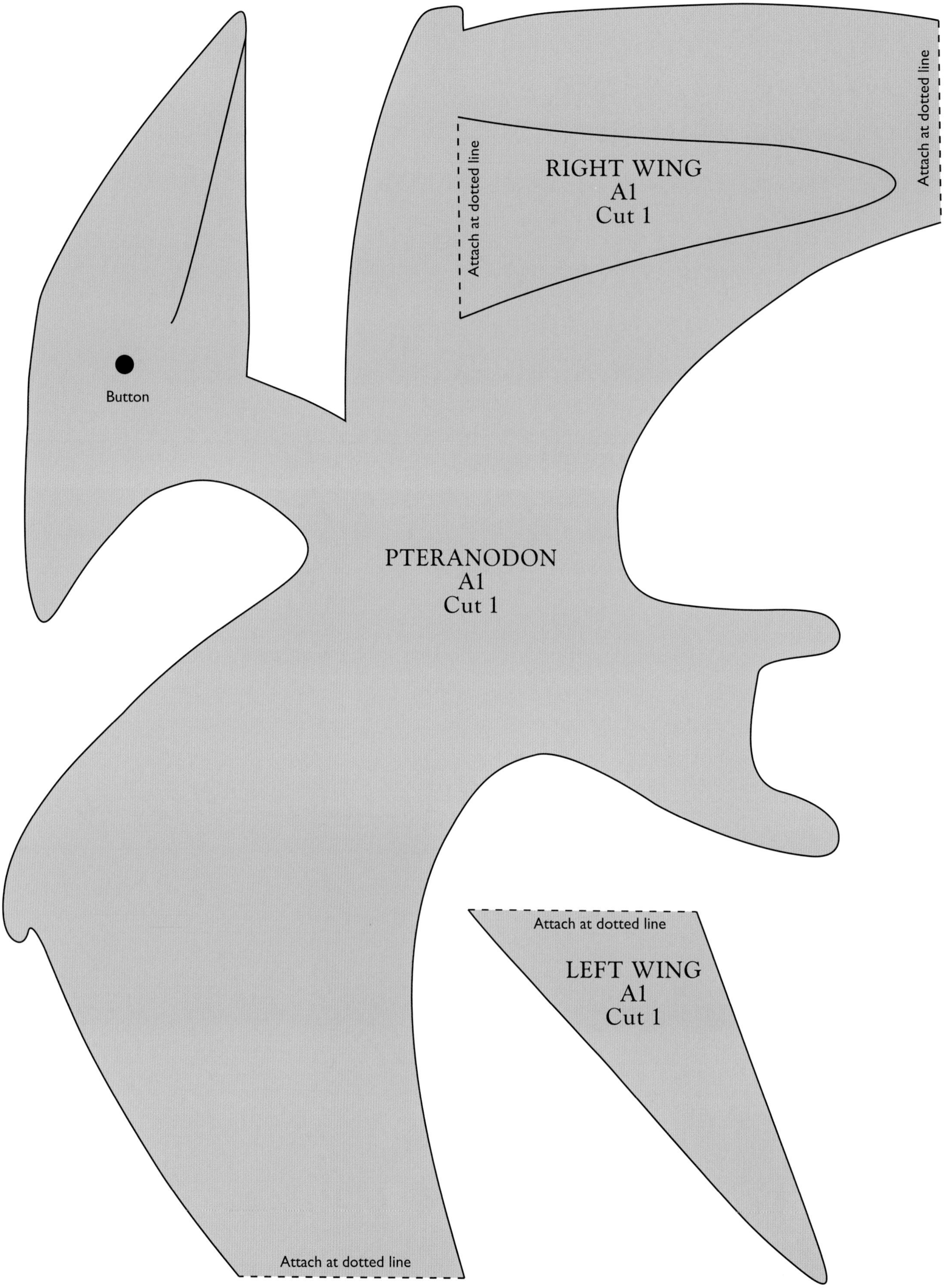

RIGHT WING
A1
Cut 1

Attach at dotted line

Attach at dotted line

Button

PTERANODON
A1
Cut 1

Attach at dotted line

LEFT WING
A1
Cut 1

Attach at dotted line

DINOSAURS

30

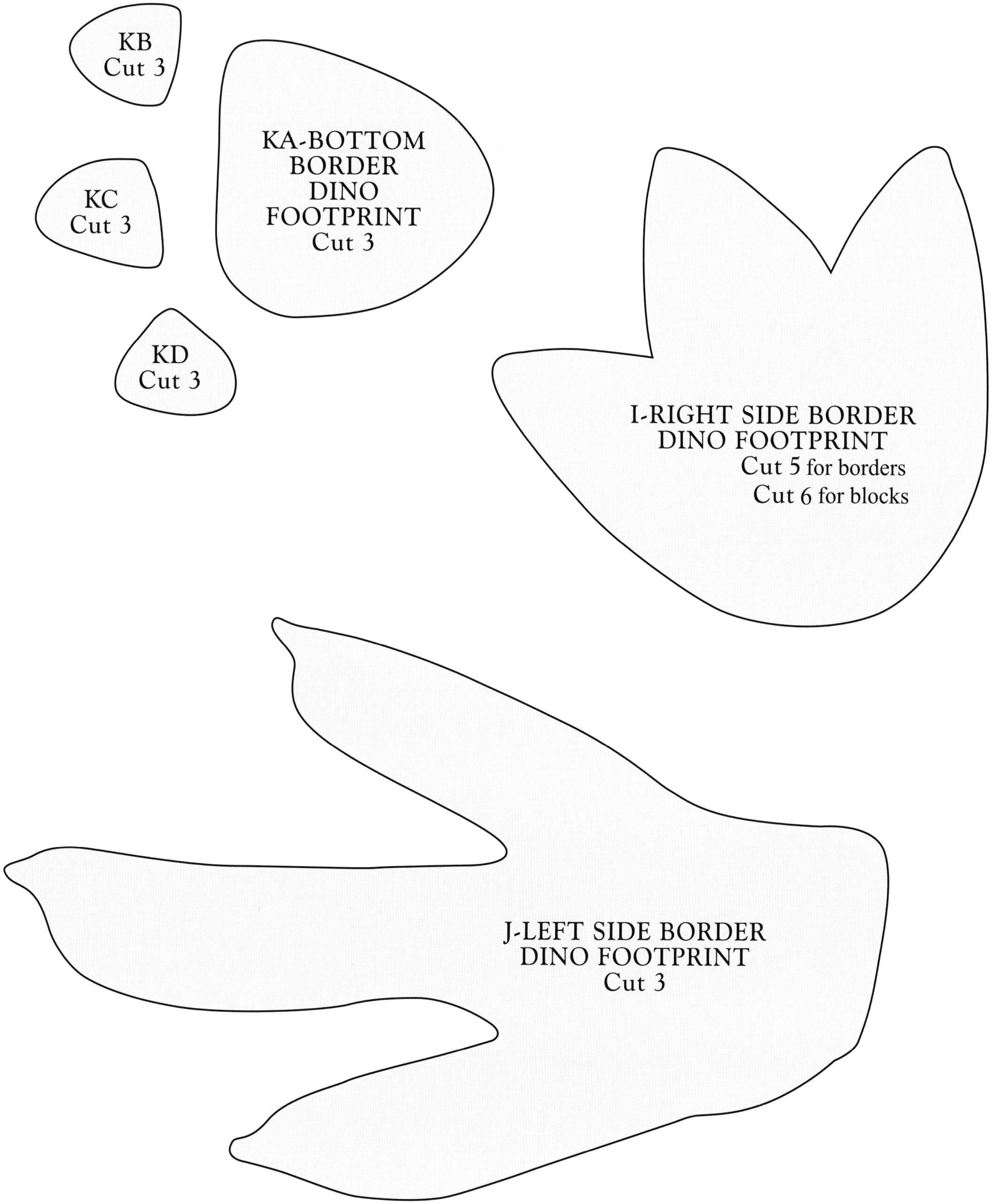

KB
Cut 3

KA-BOTTOM
BORDER
DINO
FOOTPRINT
Cut 3

KC
Cut 3

KD
Cut 3

I-RIGHT SIDE BORDER
DINO FOOTPRINT
Cut 5 for borders
Cut 6 for blocks

J-LEFT SIDE BORDER
DINO FOOTPRINT
Cut 3

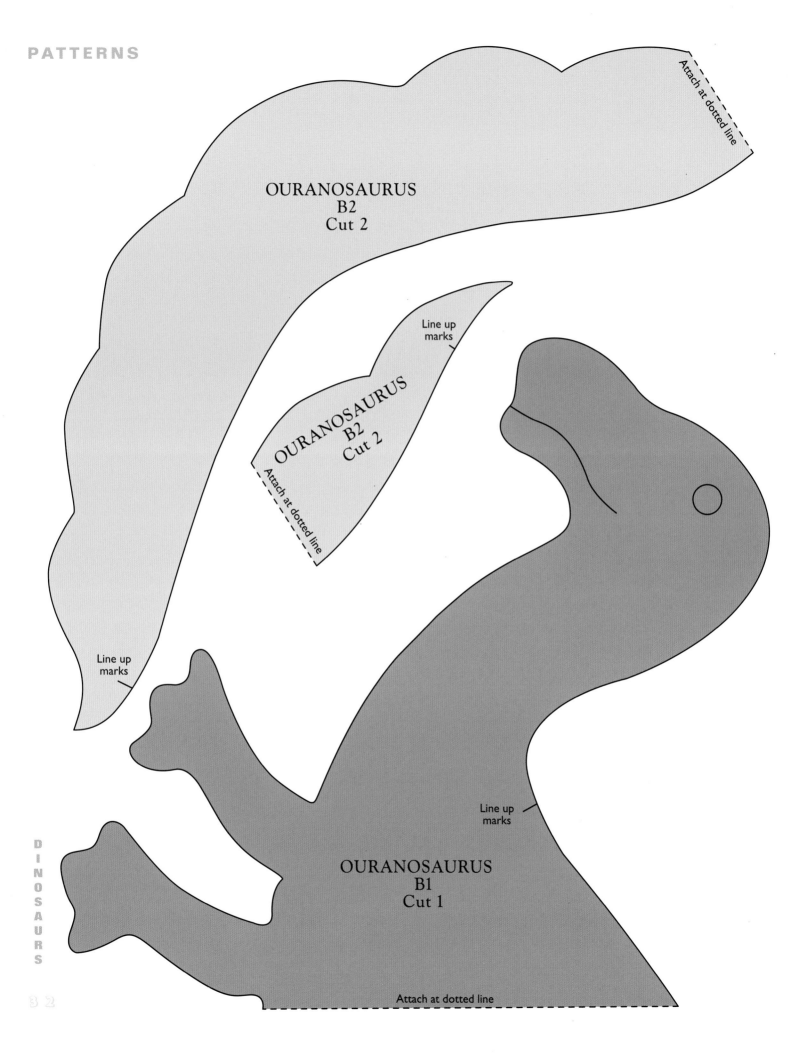

OURANOSAURUS
B2
Cut 2

Attach at dotted line

Line up
marks

OURANOSAURUS
B2
Cut 2

Attach at dotted line

Line up
marks

Line up
marks

OURANOSAURUS
B1
Cut 1

Attach at dotted line

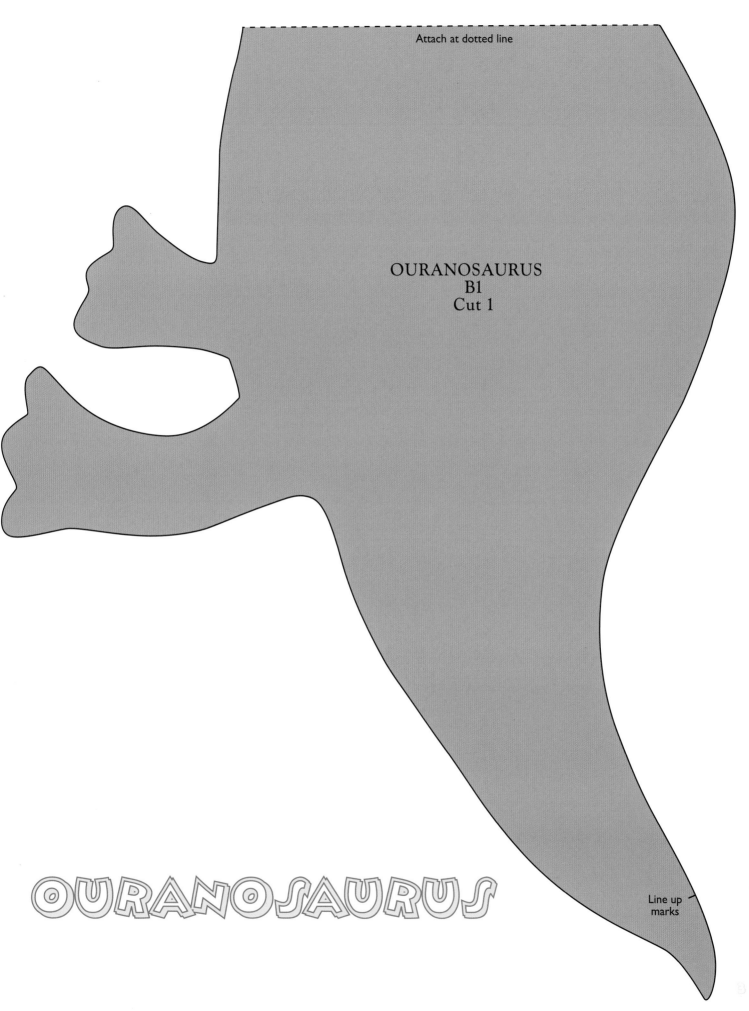

OVIRAPTOR

Attach at dotted line

OVIRAPTOR
C1
Cut 1

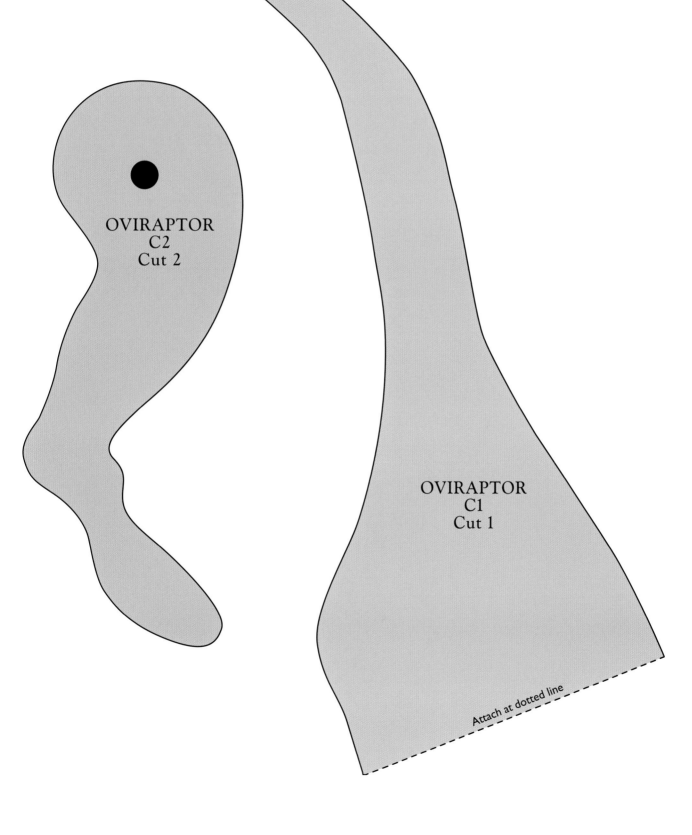

OVIRAPTOR
C2
Cut 2

OVIRAPTOR
C1
Cut 1

Attach at dotted line

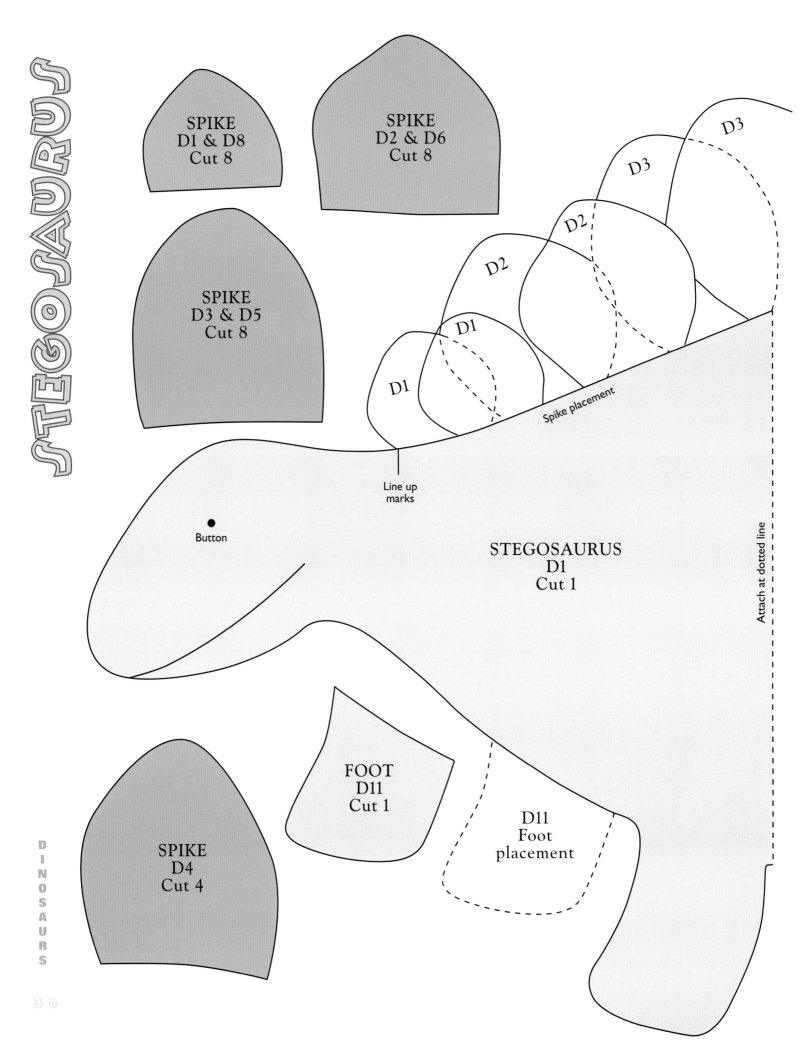

STEGOSAURUS

SPIKE
D1 & D8
Cut 8

SPIKE
D2 & D6
Cut 8

SPIKE
D3 & D5
Cut 8

D3

D3

D2

D2

D1

D1

Spike placement

Line up
marks

Button

STEGOSAURUS
D1
Cut 1

Attach at dotted line

FOOT
D11
Cut 1

D11
Foot
placement

SPIKE
D4
Cut 4

DINOSAURS

B6

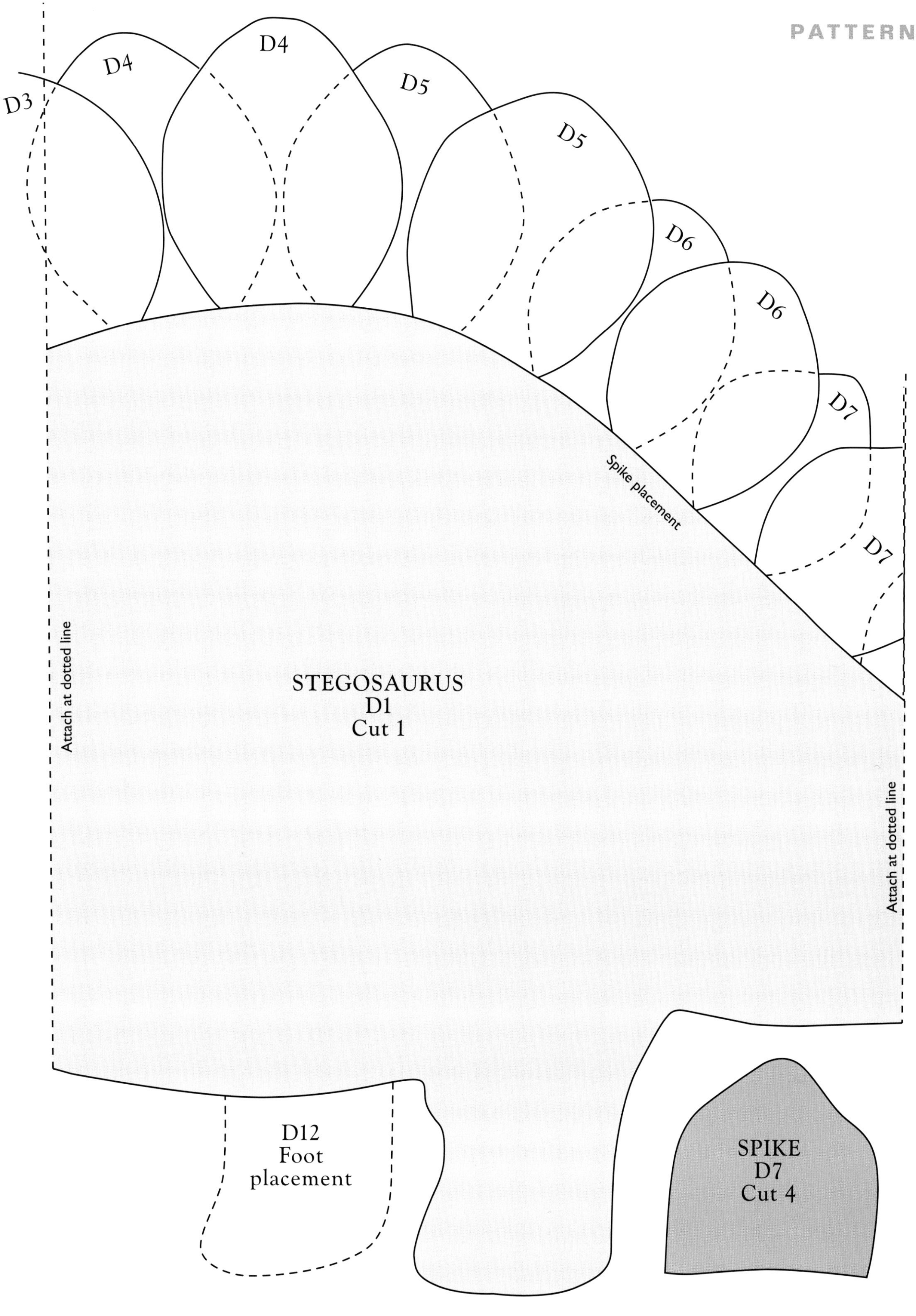

D3

D4

D4

D5

D5

D6

D6

D7

D7

Spike placement

Attach at dotted line

STEGOSAURUS
D1
Cut 1

Attach at dotted line

D12
Foot
placement

SPIKE
D7
Cut 4

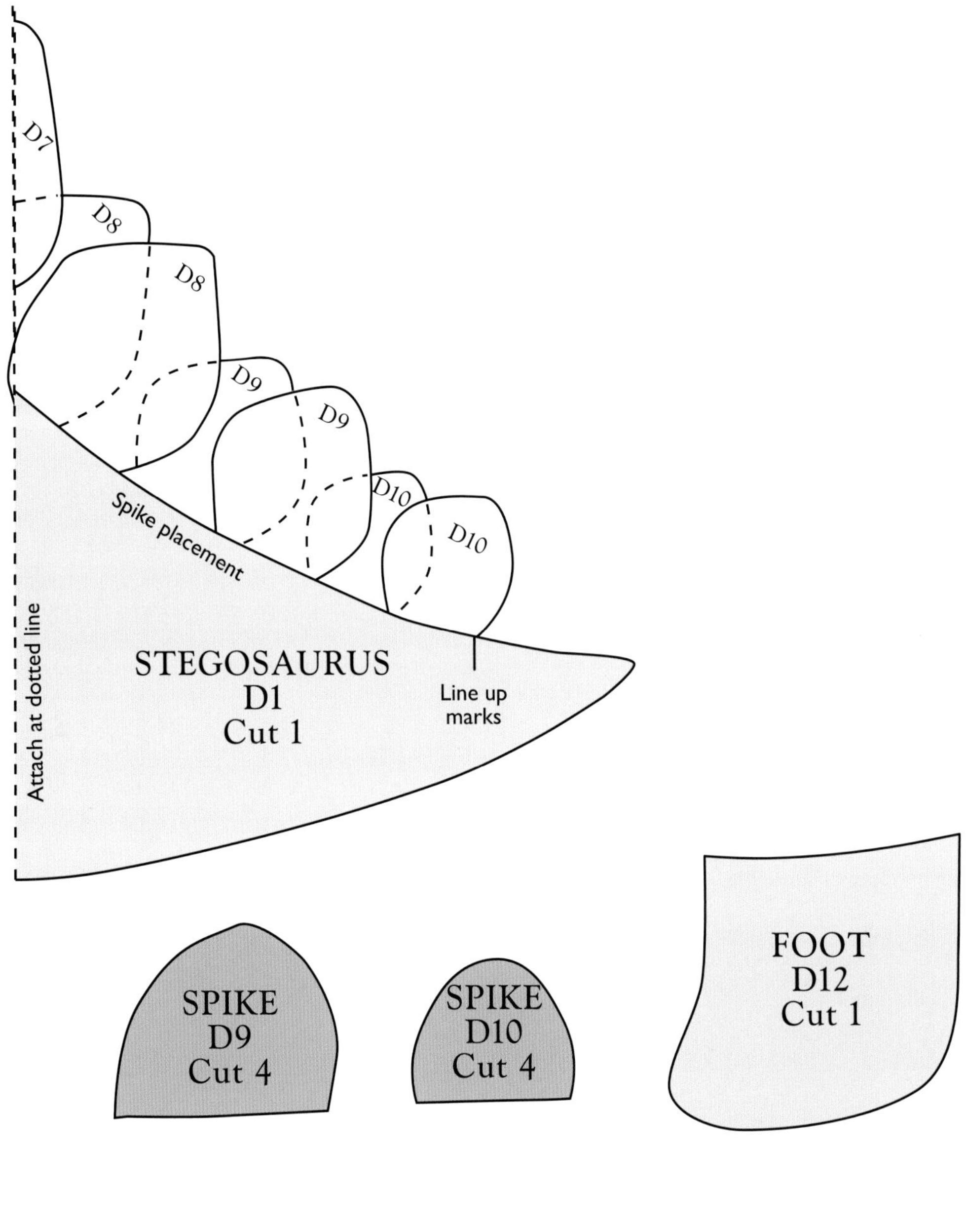

D7

D8

D8

D9

D9

D10

D10

Spike placement

Attach at dotted line

STEGOSAURUS
D1
Cut 1

Line up
marks

SPIKE
D9
Cut 4

SPIKE
D10
Cut 4

FOOT
D12
Cut 1

Gather here

M
BUG WING
Cut 8 from
doubled fabric

N
BUG
WING

M
BUG
WING

O
BUG BODY

N
BUG WING

M
BUG WING

Gather here

N
BUG WING
Cut 8 from
doubled fabric

O
BUG BODY
Cut 4

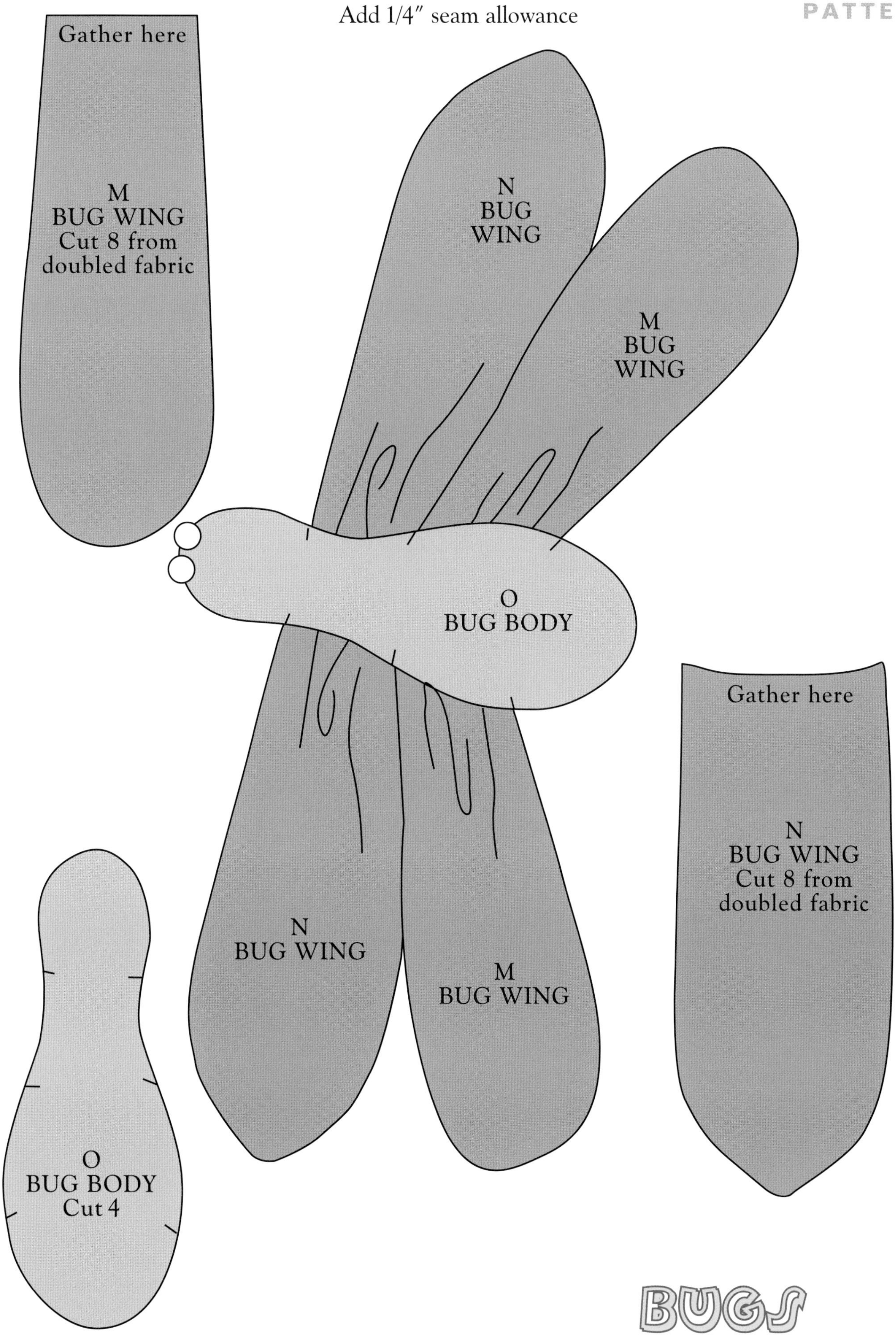

BUGS

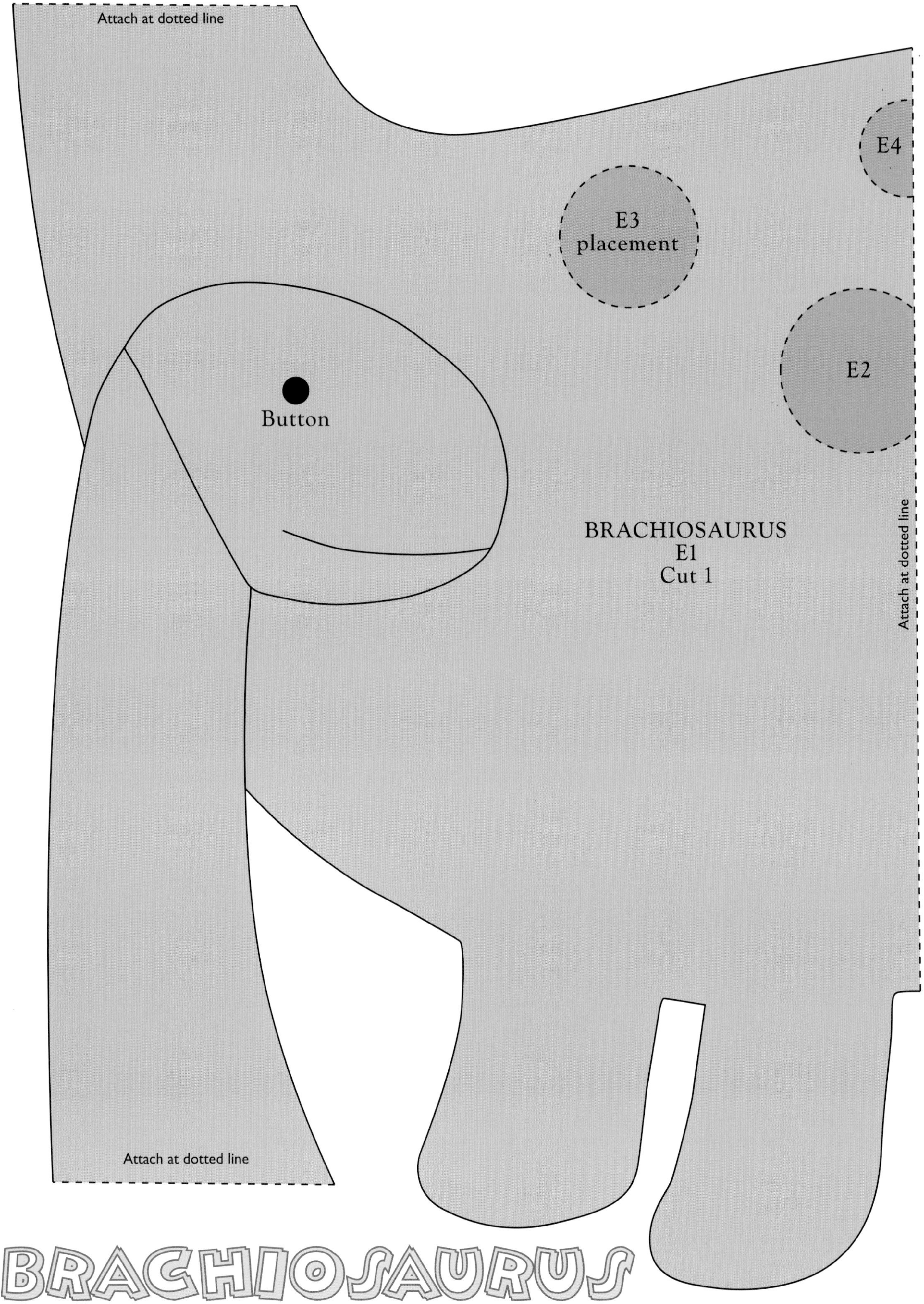

Attach at dotted line

E4

E3
placement

E2

Button

BRACHIOSAURUS
E1
Cut 1

Attach at dotted line

Attach at dotted line

BRACHIOSAURUS

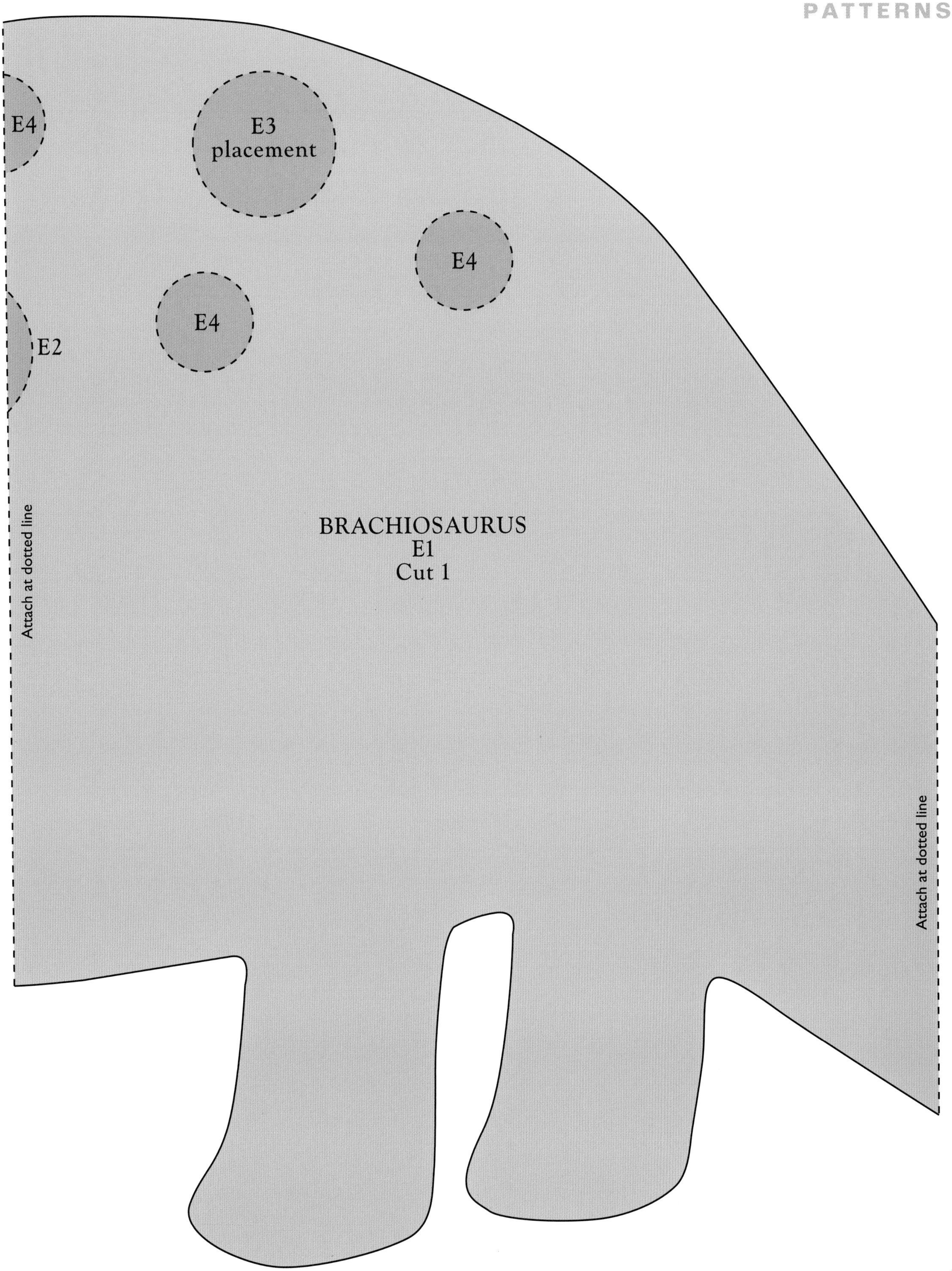

E4

E3
placement

E4

E4

E2

Attach at dotted line

BRACHIOSAURUS
E1
Cut 1

Attach at dotted line

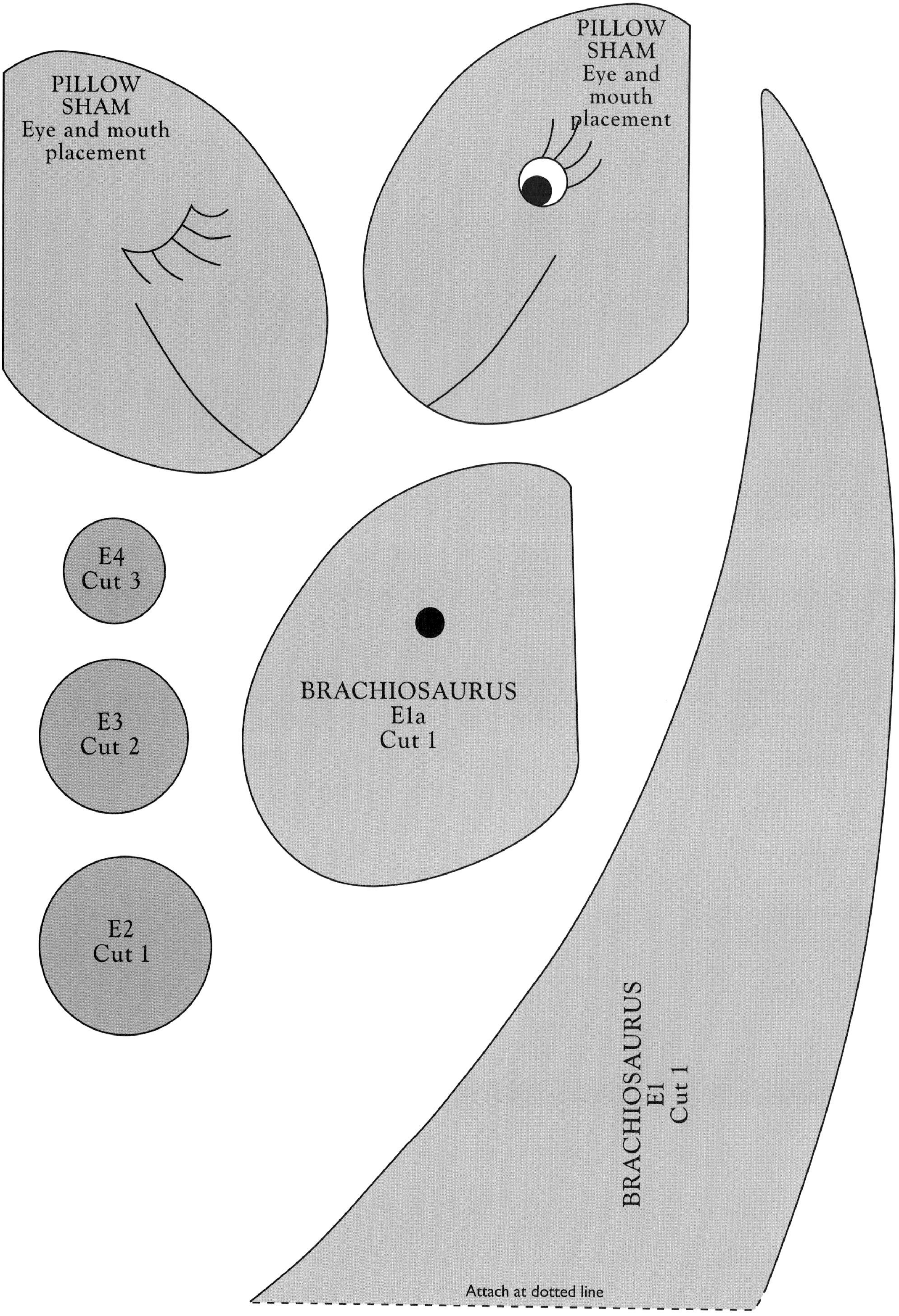

PATTERNS

PILLOW
SHAM
Eye and mouth
placement

PILLOW
SHAM
Eye and mouth
placement

E4
Cut 3

E3
Cut 2

E2
Cut 1

BRACHIOSAURUS
E1a
Cut 1

BRACHIOSAURUS
E1
Cut 1

Attach at dotted line

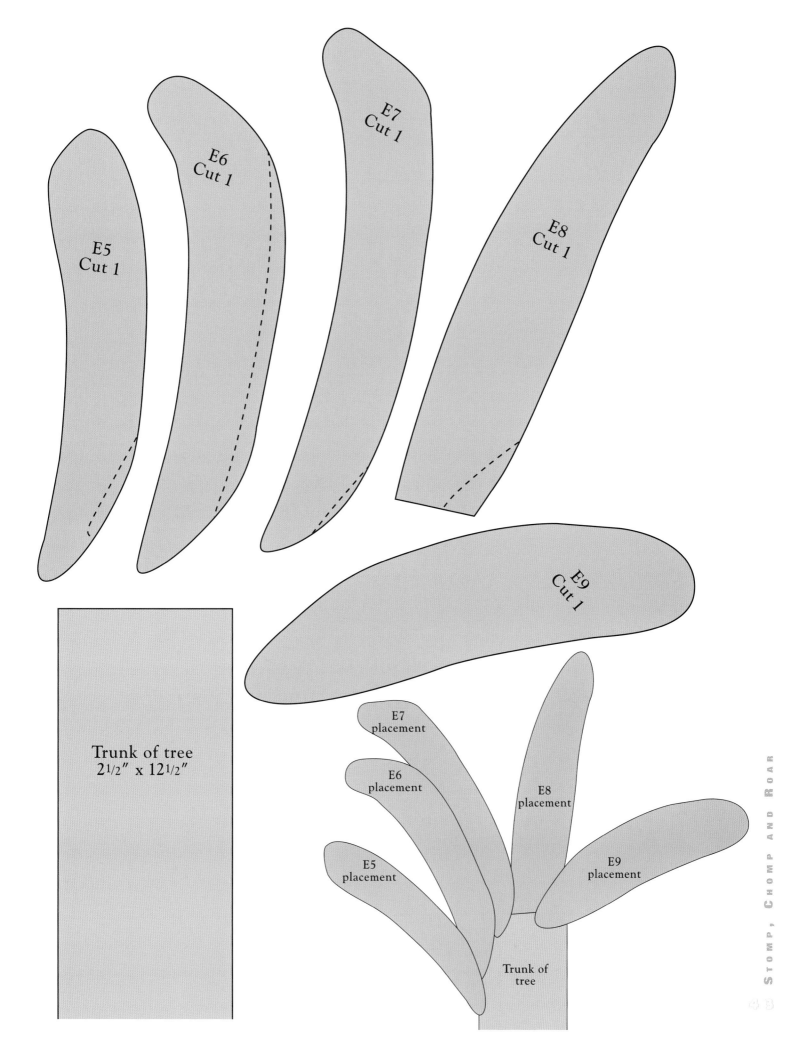

E5
Cut 1

E6
Cut 1

E7
Cut 1

E8
Cut 1

E9
Cut 1

Trunk of tree
2½″ x 12½″

E7
placement

E6
placement

E5
placement

E8
placement

E9
placement

Trunk of
tree

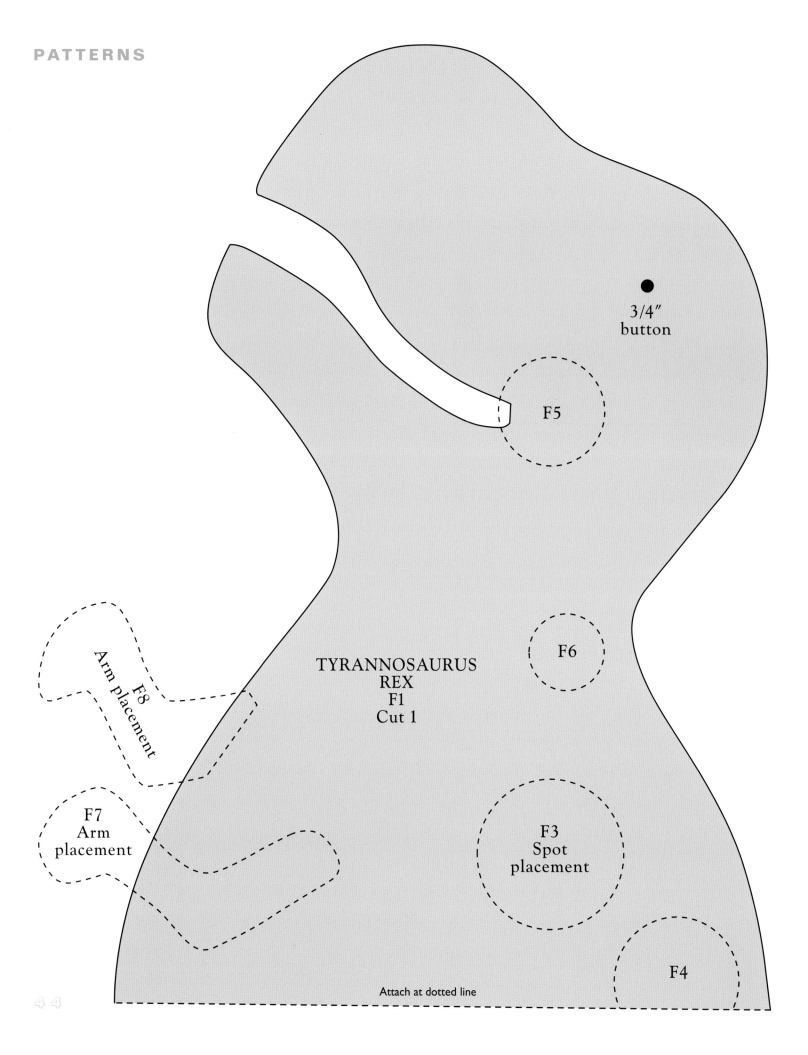

3/4"
button

F5

F8
Arm placement

F7
Arm
placement

TYRANNOSAURUS
REX
F1
Cut 1

F6

F3
Spot
placement

F4

Attach at dotted line

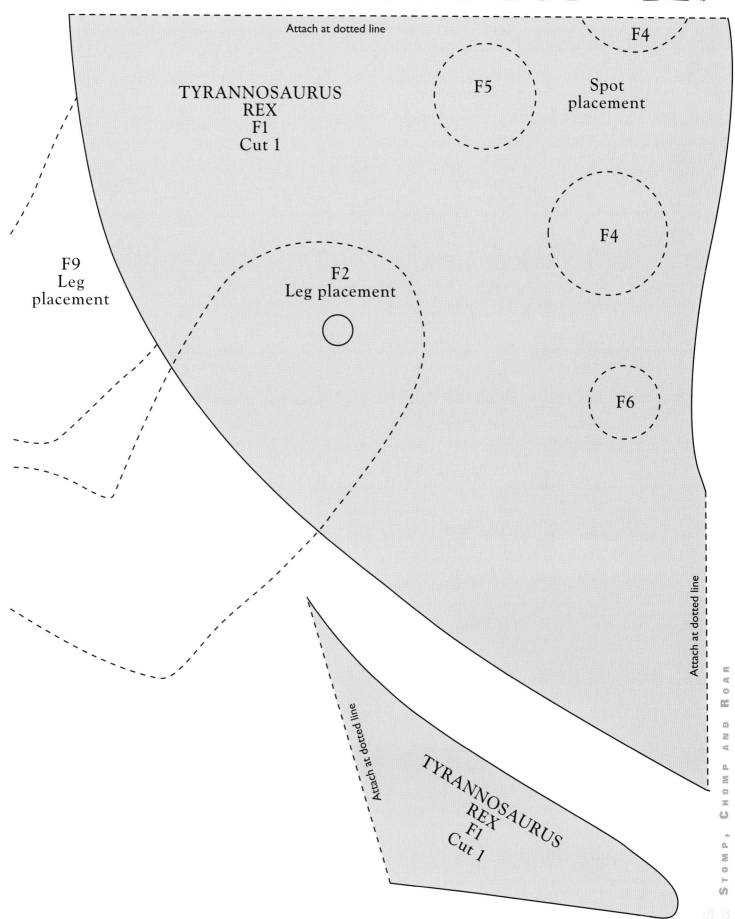

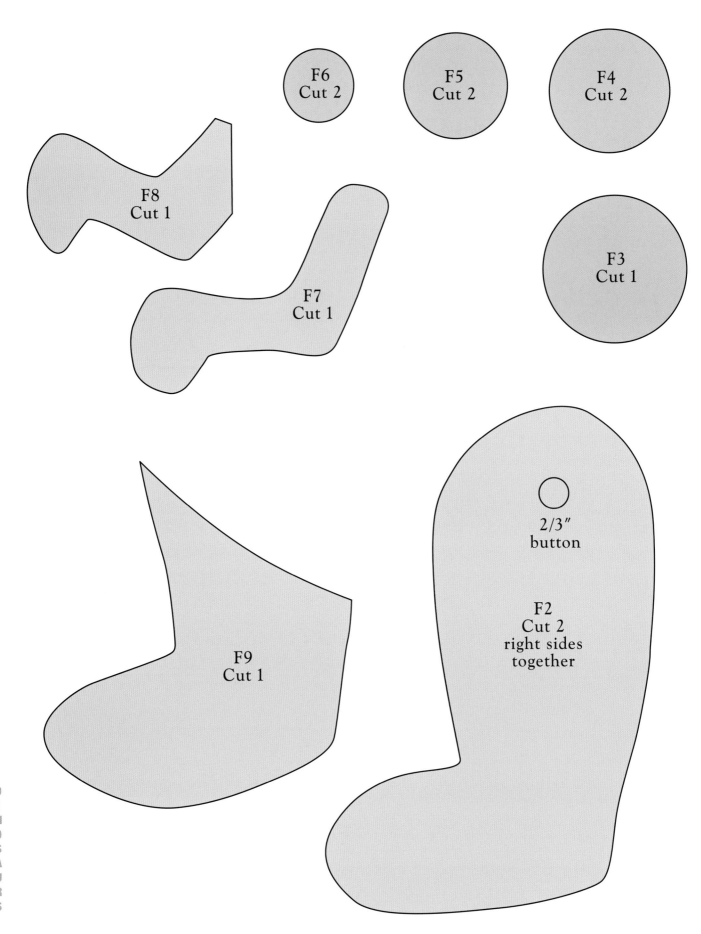

TRICERATOPS

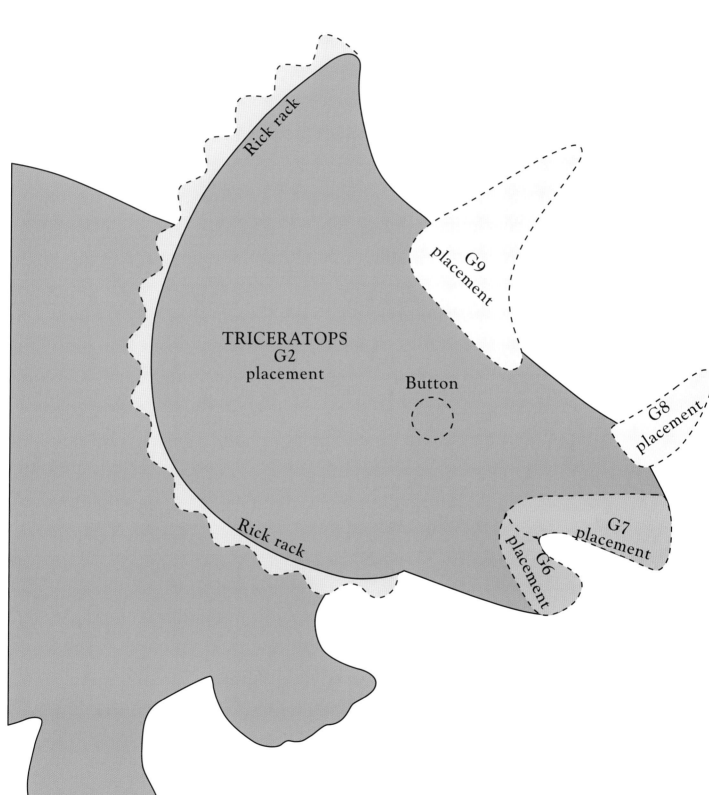

Rick rack

G9
placement

TRICERATOPS
G2
placement

Button

G8
placement

Rick rack

G6
placement

G7
placement

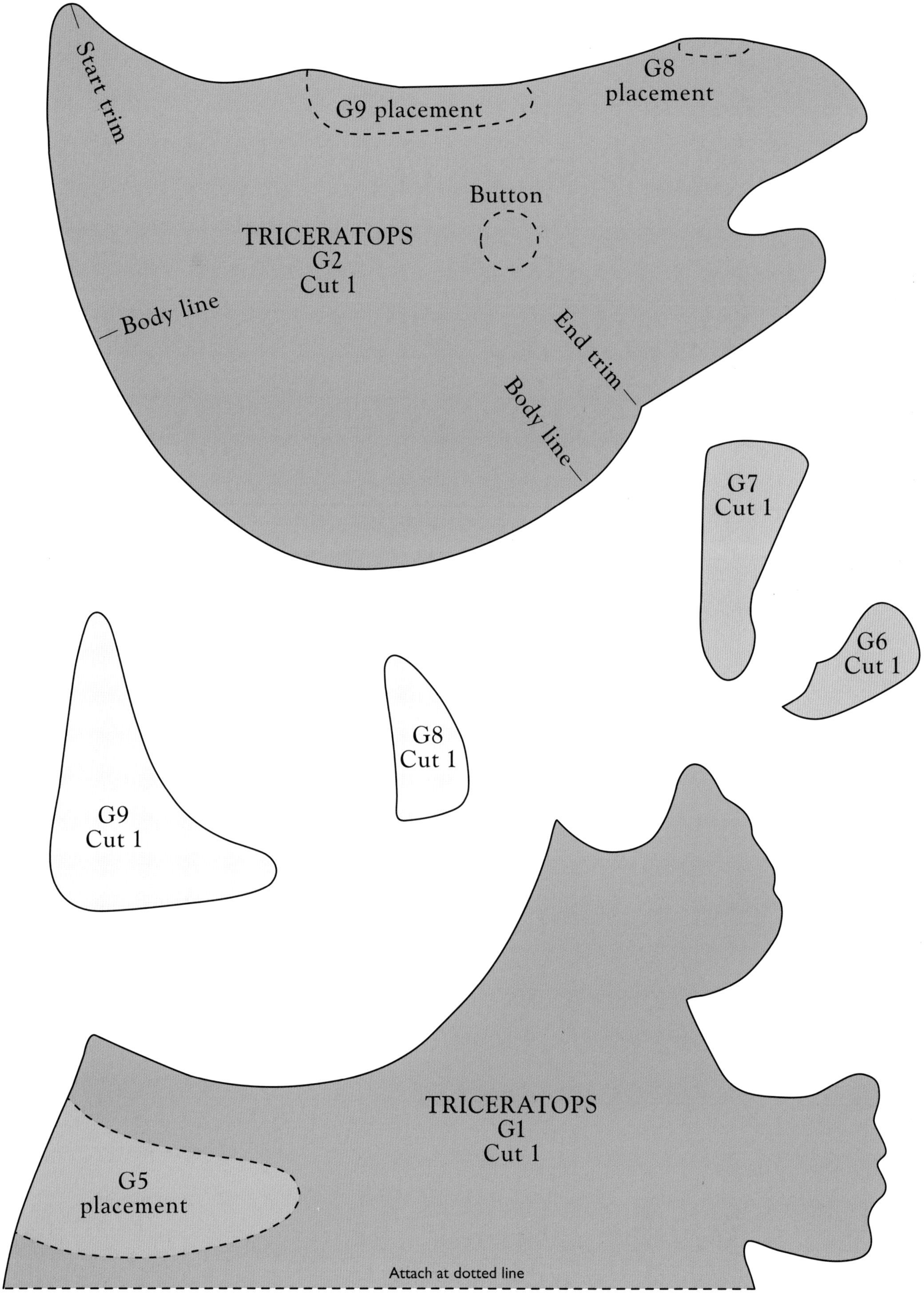

Start trim

G9 placement

G8
placement

Button

TRICERATOPS
G2
Cut 1

Body line

End trim

Body line

G7
Cut 1

G6
Cut 1

G9
Cut 1

G8
Cut 1

TRICERATOPS
G1
Cut 1

G5
placement

Attach at dotted line

TRICERATOPS

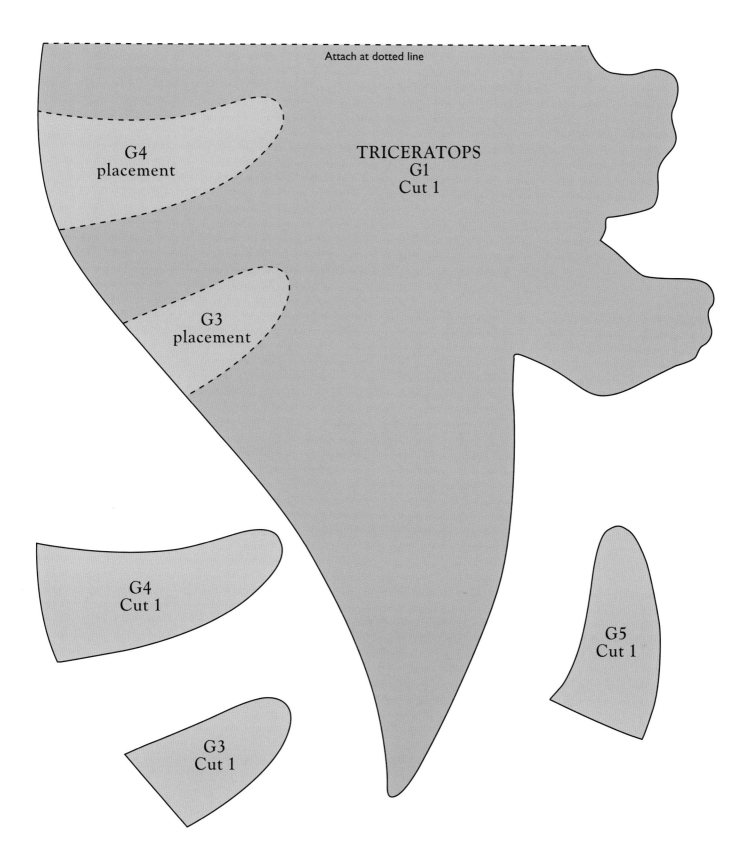

Attach at dotted line

G4
placement

TRICERATOPS
G1
Cut 1

G3
placement

G4
Cut 1

G5
Cut 1

G3
Cut 1

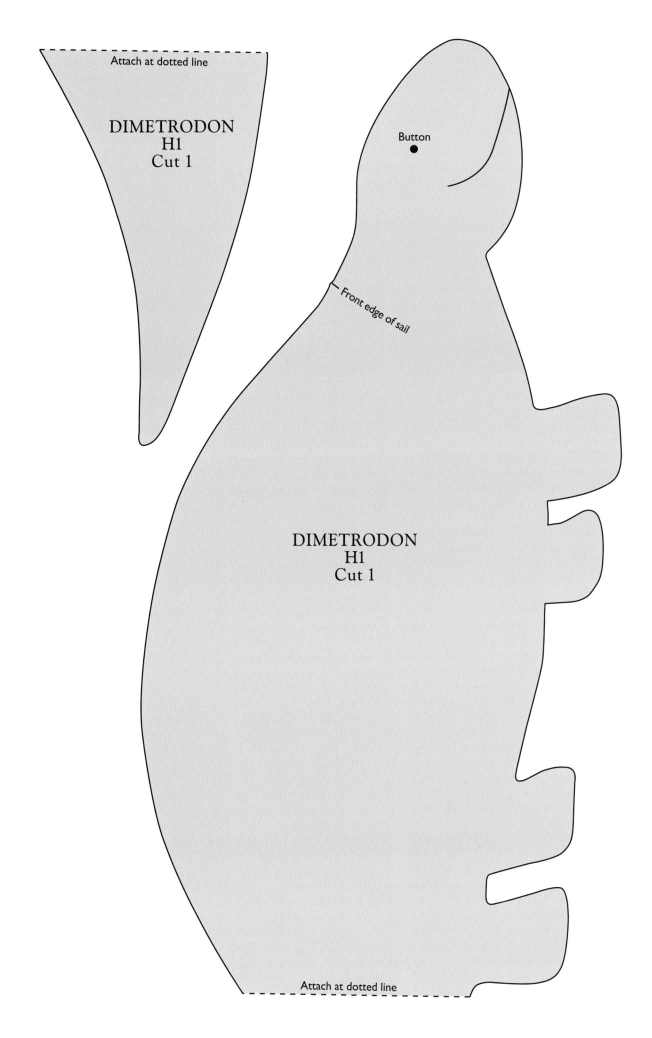

DIMETRODON
H1
Cut 1

Attach at dotted line

Button

— Front edge of sail

DIMETRODON
H1
Cut 1

Attach at dotted line

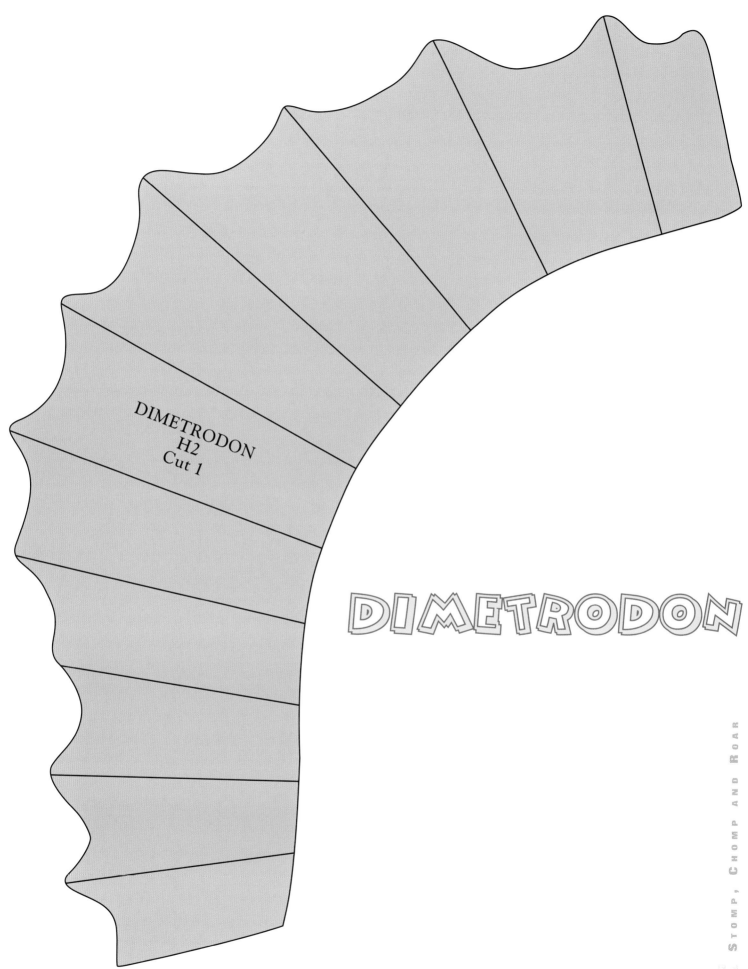

DIMETRODON
H2
Cut 1

DIMETRODON

D

Cut 1

I

Cut 1

P

Cut 2

O

Cut 4

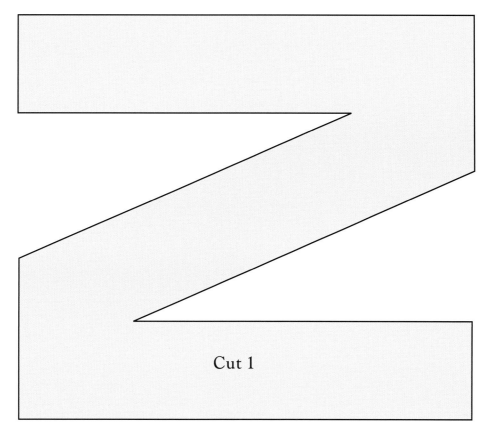

Cut 3

Cut 2

Cut 1

Cut 1

Cut 1

Cut 3

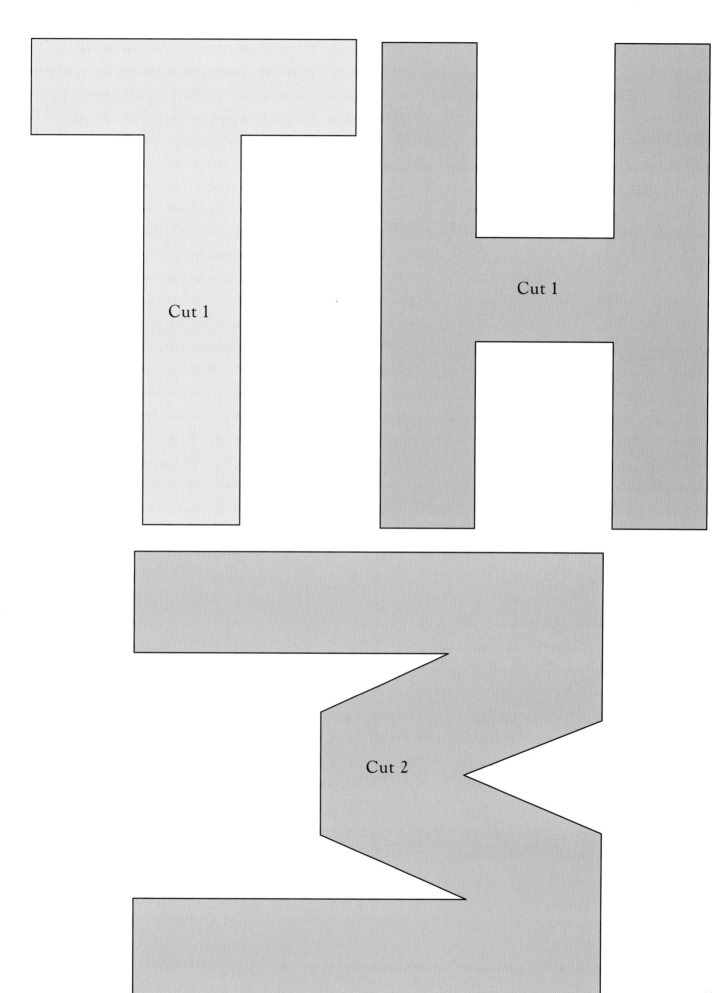

Cut 1

Cut 1

Cut 2

PILLOW SHAM

Finished size is 21 ½" X 30 ½"

FABRIC REQUIREMENTS

- ⅝ yard tan for background
- 1 ½ yards black for inner border and backing
- ¼ yard green for outer border
- ½ yard brown for dinosaur
- ⅔ yard muslin
- Scraps of brown and red for bug
- 22" x 31" batting
- #12 Perle cotton for Big Stitch quilting
- Scrap of black 3-ply embroidery floss for mouth and eye
- Two 2/0 black snaps

BLOCK CONSTRUCTION

Add seam allowance on all appliqué pieces when cutting.

- Cut 1 strip 19" X 28" tan.

- From black, cut two strips 1 ½" X 18",
  two 1 ½" X 28", two 7" X 22",
  one 22" X 15 ¼", and one 22" X 13 ¼.

- Cut two 2 ½" X 18" and two 2 ½" X 31", green.

- Cut muslin 22" X 31".

- Find brachiosaurus pattern pieces on pages 40-41.

- Cut one reverse of E1 (assemble pattern) and
  one E1a from brown.
  (Head is three-dimensional.)

- Sew E1 and E1A (head), right sides together
  from one side of the line around to the other side
  of the line.

- Clip to seam and trim any bulk. Turn right side out
  and press well. Appliqué sleepy face on one side of
  Dino and the happy face on the other side with black
  3-ply floss as on pattern pieces, page 42.

- Appliqué red E2, E3s and E4s (spots) to the dino as on pattern piece.
- Appliqué E1 dino to center of background, tan.
- Find bug pattern pieces on page 39.
- Fold your red fabric with the right sides together. Cut 2 each (4 total) of wings M and N adding a ¼″ seam allowance. Sew a ¼″ seam around the curve following next to the freezer paper seam. Clip curve, trim bulk and turn right side out. Press. Baste each end and gather to ⅞″. (Keep M and N separate.)
- Cut one O body from brown scrap.
- Appliqué bug body O over the top of wing ends (see pattern for placement) between the upper left hand corner and the dino rump. Sew on snap eyes.
- Trim block to 18″ X 27″.
- Fold both black 1 ½″ X 18″ strips in half lengthways, wrong sides together, and press. Sandwich black, cut edge between a green strip 2 ½″ X 18″ and the 18″ edge of tan background, right sides together and stitch a ¼″ seam. Press to the outside with the seam allowance toward the background.
- Fold both black 1 ½″ X 28″ strips in half lengthways and press. Turn wrong side out and stitch a ¼″ seam on short ends. Turn right side out and press. Pin to the background matching up with black on each end. Pin green 2 ½″ X 31″ over the top right sides facing the background. Stitch ¼′ seam. Press to the outside with seam allowance toward background. Stitch the black ends of the top and bottom tabs to the green.
- Cut muslin and batting 22 ½″ X 31 ½″.
- Sandwich the batting between the front and the muslin. Baste in place.
- Quilt sham with Big Stitch as desired.
- Trim batting and muslin to front 22″ X 31″.

Back of Sham

- Fold and press black 7″ X 22″ in half lengthways to make 3 ½″ X 22″. Press ¼″ under on 22″ side. Pin the other front side of 22″ to the wrong side of a 22″ x 13 ¼″ strip. Sew a ¼″ seam. Press the seam toward the 7″ piece. Fold the side you pressed the ¼″ seam under on, down over the seam you just sewed, and pin. Stitch close to the edge and then ¼″ in from the edge. Make this piece the left side of the sham back. Pin in place on left side of front, right sides together with 3 ¼″ tab on inside.
- Repeat last step for 15 ¼″ X 22″ and 7″ X 22″ strips and pin on the right side of the front, right sides together. Left side will overlap right side tab 3 ½″.
- Sew a ¼″ seam all the way around the sham. Trim corners if needed. Serge seam (or zigzag) to keep from raveling.

Wall Hanging

- Follow directions for Pillow Sham until you get to the back of sham stage.
- After you finish the quilting on the wall hanging, finish the edge with binding and a sleeve for hanging.

Sleeve

Cut coordinating fabric 2 ½″ X 31″. Fold under ¼″ on short ends and press. Fold under ¼″ again and press and sew. Fold under ¼″ lengthways on each side and hand stitch to wall hanging.

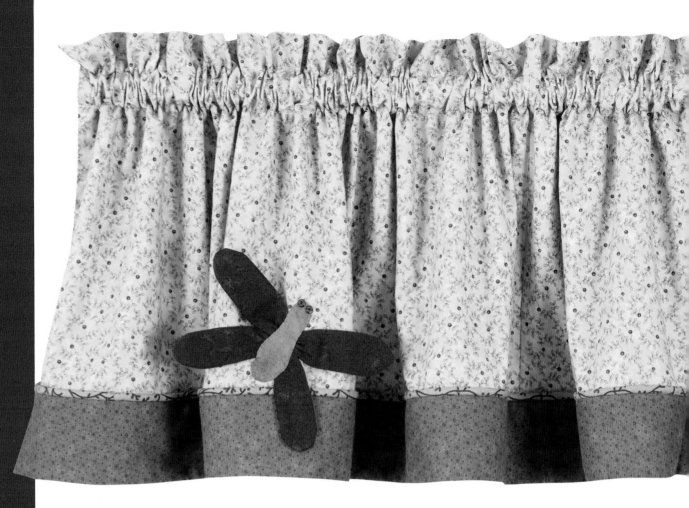

VALANCE

Finished size is 18″ X 82 ½″

FABRIC AND NOTIONS REQUIREMENTS

- ○ 1 yard tan for top
- ○ ¼ yard green for bottom trim
- ○ ⅛ yard gold for cording
- ○ 1 ¼ yards muslin for lining
- ○ Scraps red, brown and rust for bugs
- ○ 2 ⅓ yards ¼″ cording
- ○ Two size 2/0 black snaps for eyes

BLOCK CONSTRUCTION

Add seam allowance on all appliqué pieces when cutting.

For a 41″ window, I doubled the width of the window for the width of the fabric. If your window is larger, simply double the size of your window for your fabric width. You might want to add more footprints or put another bug on the right side of the curtain also. The rule of thumb is to double or triple your window width. With the cording on this curtain, you only need to double.

- ○ Cut two pieces tan 15 ½″ X 42″.
  Sew end to end with a ¼″ seam.
- ○ Cut two pieces gold 1 ½″ X 42″.
  Sew end to end with a ¼″ seam.
- ○ Cut two pieces green 4″ X 42″.
  Sew end to end with a ¼″ seam.
- ○ Cut two pieces muslin 18 ¾″ X 42″.
  Sew end to end with a ¼″ seam.
- ○ Wrap cording lengthways with 1 ½″ x 42″ gold and baste ¼″ from the edge.
- ○ Sandwich cording between top of tan and bottom of green.